THE SAVE
OF MY LIFE

THE SAVE

My Journey Out of the Dark

OF MY LIFE

COREY HIRSCH

with Sean Patrick Conboy

Collins

Published by Collins, an imprint of HarperCollins Publishers Ltd

First published by Collins in a hardcover edition: 2022
This trade paperback edition: 2023

HarperCollins books may be purchased for educational, business, or sales promotional use through our Special Markets Department.

HarperCollins Publishers Ltd
Bay Adelaide Centre, East Tower
22 Adelaide Street West, 41st Floor
Toronto, Ontario, Canada
M5H 4E3

www.harpercollins.ca

Library and Archives Canada Cataloguing in Publication
Title: The save of my life : my journey out of the dark / Corey Hirsch ; with Sean Patrick Conboy.
Names: Hirsch, Corey (Hockey goalkeeper), author. | Conboy, Sean Patrick, author.
Description: Previously published in 2022.
Identifiers: Canadiana 20230485839 | ISBN 9781443461115 (softcover)
Subjects: LCSH: Hirsch, Corey (Hockey goalkeeper) | LCSH: Hirsch, Corey (Hockey goalkeeper)—Mental health. | LCSH: Hockey goalkeepers—Mental health—Canada. LCSH: Hockey goalkeepers—Canada—Biography. | LCSH: Obsessive-compulsive disorder—Patients—Canada—Biography. | LCGFT: Autobiographies. | Classification: LCC GV848.5.H52 A3 2023 | DDC 796.962092—dc23

Printed and bound in the United States of America
23 24 25 26 27 LBC 5 4 3 2 1

To my family, to those who struggle with mental health
and to those who have lost their lives in their battle with it

I am about to drive my car off this cliff.

I am going to end my life.

I am past the point of thinking about it. It's done. I don't even have the energy to ask *why* anymore. There is only *how*. How can I make this pain go away? How can I escape from the prison of my own mind? How can I stop these ceaseless thoughts? This bottomless, bottomless, bottomless darkness. This infinite loop, loop, loop, loop, loop, loop, loop, loop, loop, loop, loop, loop, loop that is my broken brain.

I don't want to actually die—not really. Not rationally. Not if I had a choice to live a normal life. But at this point, I can't stop the thoughts. They won't negotiate with me. They don't respond to my tears or my begging. They don't listen to me. They just scream at me. They will not, will not, will not, will not, will not willnotwillnotwillnotwillnot stop.

They tell me, *You are a monster. You are worthless. You are broken. You are sick. Sicksicksicksicksicksicksick.*

I just want to be at peace. I want it more than life itself. So I am about to drive my car off this cliff at 140 miles an hour. It makes no sense at all, from the outside. On paper, my life is about as perfect as you could ever ask for. I am living all my wildest dreams. You see, all I ever wanted to be, ever since I was a little kid, was a goalie. The exact moment I saw Gerry Cheevers wearing that iconic fibreglass mask on *Hockey Night in Canada*—you know the one, with the little black stitches painted all over it—I just knew. *That's it. I know what I want to do with my life. I want to be the guy behind that mask.*

Well, somehow, some way, I actually became that guy. I became that one-in-a-million Canadian story. In February, I backstopped an underdog Team Canada to an improbable silver medal at the '94 Olympics in Lillehammer. When we got back home, I was treated like a small-time hero. Then in June, I got called up to be the third-string emergency goalie for the New York Rangers during their iconic run, and I drank champagne out of the Stanley Cup. I got to live out my wildest childhood dreams, next to guys like Mark Messier and Brian Leetch, in the greatest city in the fucking world. Can you imagine anything better?

And it meant nothing to me. Less than nothing. I didn't even stay for the legendary tickertape parade through Manhattan. I immediately got on a plane in a cold sweat and went back home to Canada so that I could be alone with my unrelenting, endless, endless, endless thoughts.

And that's how I got here.

It's past midnight, and I am standing on the edge of this cliff in Kamloops, British Columbia, looking out over the horizon. And nothing exists. None of those good things happened to me. None of those accomplishments. None of the warm memories or the road trips or the times I almost pissed my pants laughing.

They're vapour, man. They're *gone*. The only thing that exists in the entire universe is the recurring loop in my brain. The thoughts. On repeat, full volume, all day, every second, every nanosecond. No break.

Darkness, darkness, darkness, darkness, darkness.

I look out over the horizon in front of me—so much endless Canadian horizon—and as I stare blankly into the colourless sky, I am completely calm. I don't think of my family. I don't think of my girlfriend. I don't think of hockey. I don't think of anything, to be honest. I am empty. I get in my car. It's a 1990 Plymouth Laser with the turbo engine. Not a Ferrari, but it can fly. I turn the ignition. I rev the engine. I back up about a mile so I can get some speed. The roads are so familiar. I've been down them hundreds of times while playing junior hockey for the Kamloops Blazers. Back in the good old days, when my brain wasn't broken. Back when things made sense. I crank up the knob on the radio. AC/DC as loud as the radio can go. I grip the wheel with both hands. I don't talk to God. I don't ask anyone for forgiveness. I don't have any poetic thoughts. This is not a movie.

I just think, *Fuck it. I'm so tired. Fuck it.*

I slam my foot down on the gas and beg, *Please God, just let this all end.*

The car explodes forward. I'm in first gear, second gear, third gear . . .

I'm up to 100 miles an hour.

The G-force sucks me back into the seat. I am blank. The car is driving me. It's in control now. I am a passenger on a train to nowhere. There is nothing left to do but look out the window. So I look out the window. Trees.

I'm up to 130.

I'm genuinely very sorry to everybody—I really am. I'm *so* sorry now. I don't want to make anybody sad. I really don't. Please don't be sad. I don't want to make anybody come to my funeral. Don't come. Don't be sad about this. I don't want it to be this way. But it *is* this way, and no other way, and it will be this way until the end of time. I am so sorry. But I just can't keep going, you understand?

140.

If you knew what it was like to live inside my mind for

30 seconds, then I know you would understand. If you could hear the voices, you'd know why it has to be this way. You would know how much I just need *peace*.

I don't wanna I don't wanna I don't wanna but I have to. I . . .

The car is floating now. It's going so fast that everything feels slow. Airless. Frictionless. Trees are going so fast. Can't even see them. Blur. Little sticks whizzing by. I'm coming up to the edge of the cliff now. I can feel it. Can't see it, but I can feel it. All I see is the horizon. Sky. It doesn't get any closer or further away. It's just there. Colourless and endless. Any second now, there will simply be no road underneath me anymore. It will vanish. I will vanish. Then the thoughts will cease. I will finally be at rest.

The pedal is to the floor. I don't want to die I'm sorry I'm sorry I'msorryfuckIreallyamsorry but I can't keep going on.

Any second now. Oblivion.

Darkness, darkness, darkness, darkness, darkness, darkness.

And then—for whatever reason—this *thought* pops into my head. A new thought. A different thought. A stranger. It flashes for a brief moment in the darkness, like heat lightning way, way off in the distance. Just so faint. A tiny little bit of a glow. It is not a profound thought. It is not a message from God. It is not even particularly interesting. But for some reason, it appears out of nowhere. It snaps me out of the trance.

I slam my foot on the brake. *No no no NO NO NONO-NONONONO. Not now, not now, not now.*

The car starts skidding and skidding and skidding. My body lunges forward and hits the steering wheel. I feel the unseen forces of the world. Physics. Gravity. I suddenly feel very, very, very small. The world feels very big. We skid for what seems like forever. Trees come and go. The world is in control now. Me and the car, we're just along for the ride. The world will do with us what it pleases. We skid. We squeal. We whirl. We wonder. The pavement underneath us will either still be there, or it won't. We wait to find out.

We're sliding. We're helpless. And then, for no good reason, we stop just short of the cliff. The ground is still beneath us, somehow. The tires are smoking. AC/DC is still playing. The road and the trees and the grass and the sky are still there, just like they were before. Like nothing happened at all. We're still here, me and the car.

And all I can do is sit there in the middle of the road, sobbing and sobbing and sobbing. Begging. Pleading with whoever is out there.

Please, I think, *somebody help me. For the love of God, somebody please help me.*

1

I can tell you the exact moment when my brain broke. As a matter of fact, there are two distinct parts of my life. Everything that happened before this one fleeting moment, and everything that happened after. I had one simple, meaningless, *nothing* thought. A throwaway thought. A thing that has been thought of 100 million times by 100 million people throughout human history. It floated into my brain out of nowhere at all, and nothing was ever the same again.

It was May 6, 1994. I should have been having the time of my life. We were playing the Capitals in the second round of the playoffs, and I was the emergency goalie for the Rangers. No pressure. No expectations. No Twitter. Just a front row seat to a historic Stanley Cup run. What a job, right?

We were already up 3–0 in the series, and this being the '90s, I went out to a bar in DC with a couple of our other "black aces"—the emergency players, the guys in the suits watching from the luxury boxes. We were standing around the bar having a couple beers with a few of the Capitals' black aces, who were there as well. It was a different era. We were just shooting the shit. Nothing crazy. I wasn't drunk. Wasn't even buzzed. Wasn't in a bad mood. I was just standing there with a Coors Light in my hand, looking around the bar, when this strange *thought* arrived. This random, meaningless, dark thought came floating into my brain. And nothing—and I mean nothing—in my life was ever the same again.

It felt like my brain had short-circuited. And I don't mean that as a metaphor. I mean it literally. I mean it *physically*. The best way that I can describe it is that it actually felt like somewhere deep, deep, deep within my subconscious, an electric wire had snapped, and my brain was on fire.

One second, I was *me*. The next second . . .

Dark, dark, dark, dark, dark, fear, fear, fear, worry, darkness, darkness, darkness, they'll know, they'll find out, why are you even thinking that? Why, why, why, darkness, darkness, walls are closing in, they know, they know, they know, they know, *they can tell, your life is going to crumble, it's going to* crumble, *it's already crumbling, dark, dark, dark, dark, dark, dark, they can tell, they can tell,* everyone *can tell. The worst thing that you can think of is going to happen. It is* going *to happen, any second now. The worst, the worst, the worst, dark, dark, dark.*

Endless. Endless, endless, endless. Bottomless. No time, no space, no beers, no friends, no teammates, no hockey, no inside jokes, no laughter, no tomorrow or later today or anything at all. Nothing exists except the thought itself. The thought itself is here, and it's never going away. You don't exist. Only the *thought* exists, forever, on a loop.

And now you might be wondering, My God, what *was* the thought? What kind of thought could make a seemingly "normal" person spiral out of control, out of nowhere, in the middle of a bar, surrounded by his buddies?

Well, you know what's really interesting? The exact thought itself doesn't matter.

When you are sick like I was sick, you eventually learn that there are a million versions of the dark thought. There are a million variations, depending on the person. But just try this: I want you to close your eyes and think of the thing that is most horrifying to you. I'm not joking. Think of all your dreams and hopes, and then think of something that could take it all away in an instant. I mean, really go as deep as you can. Think of something that's so terrible that it almost makes you physically sick. Now imagine that *you* are the reason for it happening. Think of the thing that you would *never* actually do in a million years.

Something probably flickered in your head just now, and it was too dark to even hold on to. You barely even let it register in your brain, because it was too much. It vanished before you even let yourself register that it arrived.

Have you ever been driving down a two-lane highway on a beautiful day, and maybe your family is in the car with you, or your best friend, and you don't have a care in the world? Life is amazing. When all of a sudden, out of nowhere, this horrific thought comes drifting into your mind?

What if . . . what if I just turned the steering wheel ever so slightly?

What if I just drifted off into the oncoming lane? It wouldn't take any effort at all. A flick of the wrist, and I'd be gone.

What if . . .

Where did that thought even come from? You didn't *think* to think it, right? It just slithered out from some dark rock in the corner of your subconscious. The thought was not yours. You don't want to do that. In fact, it's the most terrifying thing that you can think of. And yet . . . the thought arrived anyway.

Why?

The variations of the darkness are limitless, and they often prey upon the things you hold most dear in the entire world.

Maybe you're a new parent, and you love your child more than anything in the world. You love your newborn baby more than life itself. You love them so much that sometimes when you look at them, your heart feels like it's going to explode.

So how come you just had this fleeting, ridiculous, absurd thought, a thought so dark that it makes you physically sick?

What if . . .

What if I hurt my child?

Millions of people have these random, dark, sickening thoughts, and then they're gone. They stare into the abyss for a millisecond—not because they actually *want* to do that thing at all, but because the thought of it horrifies them so much that they can't help but notice the thought and find a dark fascination in it. Then—*snap*—in an instant, it's gone. Before they can ever internalize the darkness, it's all over. They turn the radio on. They think of the laundry they have to do when they get home. They snap right back to reality, and the abyss fades away.

Ha. Phew. What the hell was that?

But what if you had one of those random dark thoughts, and then when you went to turn the radio on, or think about your laundry, or think about anything else at all . . . it didn't work? What if you couldn't look away from the abyss? What if your thoughts got *stuck*? We take for granted that our thoughts will go away. Eventually, they'll slowly dissolve. But what if they *don't*? What if that sickening thought got jammed up, and it played on a loop, for infinity? Even when you were taking a shower or lying down in bed at night or trying to watch TV. What if it simply never stopped? What if some wire snaps in your subconscious, and you are stuck in your mind with that sickening, horrible, worst-case scenario playing on repeat, 24/7, 365?

Well, that's exactly what happened to me on May 6, 1994.

The thought could simply not be paused. It could not be reasoned with. It would not leave. It repeated over and over again. And the really sinister part about it was that it wasn't *just* the thought itself that was the problem. It was that every time it repeated, right along with it came a tsunami of shame, panic and anxiety. To be clear, I had definitely felt anxiety before. I mean, think about my job. I was an NHL goalie. We stand in the net, all alone, in front of 15,000 screaming fans, and try not to embarrass ourselves. Anxiety was no stranger to me. But this was a whole different beast. This was anxiety on steroids. I felt cold and clammy. I started to sweat. The dark words kept repeating over and over. My brain was a broken record player.

The never-ending loop went like this:

1. The dark thought
2. A tsunami wave of anxiety, panic and confusion
3. Arguing with my brain and defiantly fighting back
4. A moment of relief
5. Original thought again

And then my internal monologue was something like this:

1. Whoa, what the hell was that? You're insane for having this horrible thought!
2. Wait, what the hell is wrong with you, anyway? Where is this stuff coming from?
3. But I don't actually want to do this! That's why I can't stop obsessing over it! I'm obsessed with the idea that I'd even have this dark thought in the first place, so of course I can't stop thinking about WHY I'm thinking it!
4. Okay, smart guy, so if you don't *really* want to have these thoughts, then why can't you *stop* thinking about it? Just stop!
5. But I can't!!!!

Imagine that argument playing out, over and over and over.

Now, it's important to understand that the first night this happened, back when this was all new to me, I had absolutely no idea what I was experiencing. It's almost like getting punched in the face repeatedly before you even know you're in a street fight. It was totally overwhelming. Inside the bar, I started to panic. I made up some lame excuse to my teammates and I got out of there as fast as I could. On my way back to the hotel, I was trying to reason with myself. I was thinking, *Okay, you probably just need some sleep. Maybe you're exhausted. Once you get some rest, this will all be over. It won't come back in the morning.*

I got back to my room and lay down and stared at the ceiling for hours. I distinctly remember that my last thought as I was finally drifting off to sleep was . . .

This is never going away.

I woke up the next morning and immediately scanned my brain for the thoughts, and within seconds, they started up again. Not only were they there, but it felt like they were now screaming at me, hitting me over the head with a sledgehammer. I literally felt like the floor was shaking.

What is that? I thought. *Is there an earthquake? In DC??? Is there a train rolling by or something? What the hell is that?*

I had no idea at the time, but it was actually my anxiety. It was so intense that my body felt as though the floor was quaking. I had absolutely no idea what was going on with my brain at the time, but all I knew was that I had to buy some time to figure out the puzzle in my head—and most importantly, more important than anything in the world in fact, was that I had to *hide it* from everyone.

I wasn't telling anyone about what I was feeling. You would've probably had to torture me to tell you what I was going through, honestly. This was *1994*, remember. I grew up in the culture of hockey, and everything I learned about being a man was taught to me on a ratty old bus rolling around the plains of Canada with 20 other guys between the ages of 16 and 20. We were taught to never, under any circumstances, talk about our feelings. You never show public affection. You never, ever, *ever* cry. If you're going through something at home, or with your girlfriend? You deal with it yourself.

Help was considered weak. A man doesn't ask for help. A real man goes through the darkness alone, and doesn't complain.

(What a crock of shit that was, eh?)

So I suffered by myself. Every day, every second, every moment, 24 hours a day, seven days a week. Repetitive, distressing *what if?* thoughts. The only time I had peace was when I was on the ice or asleep. Otherwise, the thought never left. The best way to describe the anguish is to imagine having a friend put their mouth right to your ear and repeatedly say the words, "You're a monster. You're insane. You're going to hurt the very people that you love. Everyone's going to find out that you're a monster and take away your hockey career. Everything you've ever loved is going to be taken away."

Imagine those words being whispered over and over every three seconds into your ear for 10 minutes straight without stopping. Really think about what that would feel like. Okay, now imagine your friend saying those exact same words, but they're gradually getting louder and louder for another 10 minutes, until they are almost screaming directly into your ear. Okay, now imagine that feeling 24 hours a day, all day, every day, with no way to make it stop. Sometimes it was a whisper.

Those were the good days. Mostly, though, the darkness was screaming at me.

I couldn't rationalize my irrational thoughts. Sometimes when I thought I had my brain under control, the thoughts would actually morph into something new and unexpected. At breakfast, I would pick up a knife just to put some butter on my toast, and I'd think, *Whoa, whoa, whoa, don't touch that knife, man. Don't even look at it. What if you picked it up and just snapped? What if you stabbed one of your teammates with it?* It was horrifying, repulsive. I can't stress that enough. It wasn't a fantasy. It was a nightmare. It wasn't "I *want* to do this." It was, "Oh my God, *what if* I did this?"

It made no sense, and yet I could not make it stop.

Most of the time, my thoughts had a similar underlying theme. It was usually something that was sexually intrusive, something with a stigma attached to it that could ruin my hockey career. And this is where I need the reader to be very open to what I am saying, and patient with me, because this part is really sensitive and easy to misinterpret. It would start off with a thought that I'm sure 99.9 percent of the population has had in their life. It was just a passing thought somewhere in the back of my brain: *Hey, that guy's attractive. Yeah, he's a good-looking guy.*

Now, I can already feel some people pulling away here. We're so conditioned in our society—especially in the hockey community—to recoil from complicated conversations like this. But just stick with me here.

I'd see somebody, and I'd have that simple thought.

Hey, there's a handsome guy.

But then my brain would just spiral out of control. It would go, *Hey, why did you think that? Are you attracted to him? Are you gay? Are you secretly gay, and you've been lying to yourself all this time? You must be gay to have thought that. You're gay and everybody on the team is going find out. They're going to find out, they're going to find out they're going to find out*

    they're going to find out

    they're going to find out

    they're going to find out

    they're going to find out

    they're going to find out

    they're going to find out

they're going to find out

they're going to find out

They probably know

They know

They know they're going to find out

they're going to find out

they're going to find out

they're going to find out

They know they're going to find out

They know

They know

They know

They know They knowThey knowThey knowThey knowThey knowThey know.

That's just a little snapshot inside my brain. But I'd have to fill 4,000 pages to give you the full picture. That cycle would last for hours, days.

And this is really hard to talk about, because historically, there has been so much homophobia in the sports community and in society at large, and that absolutely breaks my heart. The last thing that I want to do is to feed into that in any way. But if you want to understand what was happening in my brain, I have to take you all the way there. And to take you all the way there, I have to be honest about the times. This was 1994. Being outed as a gay professional athlete would have been a death sentence, back then. So my brain seized on that irrational fear and spun it out of control.

Now, as a 50-year-old man looking back on all of this, who has done a lot of therapy, I understand that I am not gay. Sexuality is completely beside the point, in fact. If it had turned out that I was gay, and just confused about it, that would have been an enormous relief to me. I would have had an answer for all of my confusion and suffering, and I would've been the happiest person in the world. Forget my career. Forget what anybody thought. If that was the answer, I would have embraced it and never looked back.

But that wasn't it. What was actually happening was a lot more complicated than my sexuality. My brain was just latching on to anything and everything that could take away my dreams and ruin my career or hurt the people that I loved.

In my out-of-control anxiety, if I was gay, and my teammates found out, they'd kick me off the team and I'd never play in the NHL again. They'd ostracize me and I'd lose everything I ever loved. It was just one of many irrational fears that my mind would seize onto. That was the twisted way that my brain worked. And as soon as I rationally thought my way through one obsession, my brain would just latch on to something else.

"Oh, you're not actually gay? Well guess what? You have HIV."

You see, this was all happening at the height of the AIDS epidemic, and unfortunately there was a lot of misinformation and fear going on at the time, and that was a huge trigger for me. My brain would irrationally be screaming at me that I had contracted HIV through a cut, and that I was going to give it to everyone I loved by accident. In hockey, there is always someone getting cut or getting stitches. It's an almost weekly occurrence. You have to imagine—we're constantly handling sharpened steel blades. Guys are always stepping over each other in the locker room and feeling their skates to see if they're sharp enough. Players get hit by stray pucks in practice and wipe the blood right on their pants. In our sport, blood is just everywhere.

I remember not long after the night in the bar, I was walking through the locker room, and I went into the medical room to see the trainers, and my brain flared up out of nowhere. It was a full-blown panic:

Hey, what if you just touched something that had blood on it? What if they had HIV and now you have it? What if you're giving the entire New York Rangers roster AIDS and then they're spreading it to their partners? What if you gave it to your girlfriend? You're going to make her sick. She's going to die. She's going to die die die hurt hurt hurt hurt you're going to be responsible

It's your fault your fault your fault

You're gonna hurt everyone you love

You got a cut

There was blood. There was blood. Blood blood blood blood there was There was blood. You're sick. You're sick sick sick You're sick. Blood.

B

L

O

O

D

B

L

O

O

O

D

BLOOD.

BLOOD.

As ridiculous as that thought may seem, once it was triggered, there was no stopping it. I frantically tried to figure out if I had HIV, where I may have gotten it from, and how to prevent giving it to anyone else. I went through the Rolodex in my head. I obsessively tried to figure out who was married, who may have slept with who, who was sexually promiscuous and on and on and on. My head was exploding with so many irrational thoughts that even by touching doors or towels in the dressing room or just being in the same shower room as someone else, I would convince myself that I could give someone HIV.

The thing that was tearing me up inside was the *why*. Why was I having these intrusive, never-ending thoughts? What was the spark? There was no trauma or triggering incident that could explain it. I didn't have something traumatic in my childhood that I was struggling with or repressing. In a way, it almost would have been more soothing to me if I did have something traumatic that could explain it. It was just so confusing, and so crippling. It felt like my brain had decided one day, on a whim, to betray me. More than anything, it was unbelievably *exhausting*. I can't really articulate just how tiring it is to have your brain running on a loop. Every waking hour, I would get bombarded with irrational thoughts, and then of course I was spending all this mental energy just trying to *figure it all out* like it was some sort of massive jigsaw puzzle. And if I did ever get a little brief moment of peace, the anxiety would wash away and I would get a feeling of euphoria that rushed through my body—that is, until a new thought popped up 30 seconds later and it started all over again.

If I found an answer to one *what if?* thought, the darkness grabbed onto another idea and hit me even harder. It was self-inflicted torture. It was living hell.

Mentally exhausted from the battle in my own brain, I started to oversleep. I was late for team meetings, and I was fearful of even being around my teammates because my brain would get triggered and go into overdrive. I was distraught, confused, and sick. I can't imagine what they thought. Well, I can imagine, actually. They thought I was just an asshole. That's what I would've thought if I was them. "He doesn't want to be around the boys. He doesn't care. He's pissed he's third string. What a prick."

No one had any idea of the pain I was in. During that entire Rangers playoff run, I was having anxiety attacks all day long every day at the hotel. My chest was tight. The room felt like it was trembling. Something bad was going to happen, happen, happen, happen, now, now, now—okay it didn't happen yet, but it's coming, any minute, any second. It's coming, it's coming, it's coming. It's invisible. It doesn't have a name. You can't even explain what it is. But it's coming, and it's *your fault*.

Thinking about hockey or anything else was impossible. All I wanted to do was go home. I needed to come up with a solution—or, I was convinced, I was going to hurt myself. I felt like if I just got home to Calgary, then maybe something would change. If I could just get out of the madness of New York City and back to everything that was familiar to me, then maybe something in my mind would reset. Maybe I would wake up and be *me* again, like it was all some bad dream. Maybe.

But you know what is so cruel? As miserable as I was, I simply couldn't tell anyone the truth. I couldn't just up and quit for the sake of my mental health. I know that probably sounds confusing to some people now in 2021, but as bad as it was, career suicide was somehow more unthinkable than actual suicide. I couldn't bring myself to throw away my NHL dreams, even though my life had become unbearable. So I came up with a plan of escape. If I had a serious injury, then the team wouldn't have any use for me and they'd send me home for surgery.

That's when I decided I was going to break my own hand. But I needed to make it realistic, right? It had to be something I could pass off as a hockey injury, not a bar fight or self-harm. So I covertly grabbed one of the extra stick blades from around the locker room and snuck it back to my hotel. Back then, the shafts of hockey sticks were aluminum, and the blades were attached separately and made of wood. They were heavy as hell. I figured that would do the trick, and I could disguise the injury until the next day at practice, when I could take a shot to my glove side and pretend that it was the shot that broke my hand. It was the most realistic fake injury I could think of. I mean, I was absolutely desperate at that point. Anything to get home.

So I sat there at the table of the little kitchenette in some random Marriott hotel room in the middle of one of the most exciting playoff runs in Stanley Cup history, and I smashed my left hand three or four times with the blade. Just completely smashed it. It was kind of like in those Mob movies when they catch some lowlife cheating at cards and they take him in the back room to teach him a lesson, except it was just me and *me*. I Pesci'd myself.

After the fourth slash, I was about to pass out. I collapsed on the floor and held up my throbbing hand. No dice. It turns out that it's incredibly hard to break your own hand when you're 21 years old. Too much calcium. I threw the stick blade against the wall. The bruises were pretty brutal, but my bones simply would not break. I remember lying on the bed, in tears, just thinking: *You're trapped now. You're trapped in your own fucking brain.*

To be completely honest, the rest of those playoffs were a huge blur. I don't really even know how I made it to the rink every day. I'm sure I looked like a walking ghost. But once I physically stepped onto the ice for practice, I was pretty much safe, because I didn't have much to do at all. In those two months of the playoffs, I only got into the net to practise a handful of times. I can't imagine how bad I would have looked, considering the shape I was in. In hockey, there are only two nets. Mike Richter was the starter, so he took one of the nets, and Glenn Healy took the other so that he was ready in case Richter faltered or got hurt. Richter was a workhorse and stayed out to take extra shots after practice, and Glenn would pick up anything else with whichever guys were left. I would literally just stand in the corner of the rink and wait in case they needed me. I had so much time to sit and think, and that's all I ever did, day after day after day. It was a perfect storm for my brain.

At that point, the name of the game came down to just two words: *lie* and *survive*. Say anything. If someone asks what's up with you, say you have the flu. Say you've got a migraine. Lie, lie, lie. Don't let them know it's mental. I was so alone. I couldn't turn to Google to try to figure out what I was experiencing. I was too scared to talk to any of my family about what was happening. And talking to my teammates or my coaches would have meant the end of my career, no question.

During the conference final against the Devils, I went into a depression that lasted for days. I couldn't engage people in proper conversation. I was just trying to get through the day, and at the rink, I wasn't talking to anybody. I would kind of just stare right through them. A teammate came over to my stall one day after practice. I was slumped over, bags under my eyes, I must have looked like hell. He told me not to look so glum, that life was good. And I remember thinking that it was the most ridiculous thing I ever heard.

The irony is that the 1994 Devils-Rangers conference final ended up being one of the greatest series played in the history of the NHL. Ask any Rangers fan about it, they'll instantly light up and talk about where they were watching at the time, and what the city was like back then. The series was a roller coaster that went the full seven games, and then even Game 7 went into double overtime. A trip to the Stanley Cup Final was waiting at the end of every single shot on goal. Can you imagine anything more dramatic?

And you know what? I still hate to admit this even all these years later, but I will be completely honest. I was in so much anguish at the time that I was probably the only person in the Garden on that legendary night who was praying that we would lose so that I could finally go home. It was so complicated. I was dying inside, because on one hand of course I wanted my teammates to go to the Cup Final, but on the other hand, I just didn't think I could last another minute inside my own head. It was one of the strangest experiences of my life.

When Stephane Matteau scored the wraparound winner that sent us to the final, it was one of the most electric moments in hockey history, and all I was thinking way up in the players' box on the catwalk above MSG was: *Oh my God. Another two weeks of this. Another two weeks of hell.*

Around that time, my parents were really getting worried about me. You can only hide so much from your mom, right? Moms, they always just *know.* They have a sixth sense, no matter how much bullshit you throw their way. Before the final, I called her on the phone and finally broke down. I told her about all the dark, nonstop thoughts that I was having. I told her that they had taken over my life, and that I didn't know what to do. Mom was extremely supportive, but I think she just didn't know how to help me. She didn't know what to say or what it all meant. Things were going south, hard, and I was barely getting to practice, so I asked her to fly to New York to be with me. I was close to non-functional, trying to hide and survive. I needed help.

My mom flew in and I picked her up at the airport. I have no idea how I even made it there to meet her. A lot of this time period is so hazy, and has been filled in by my family over the years. I just remember that Mom was desperately trying to lift my spirits and keep me busy, but it was difficult for me to hold a conversation. How can I concentrate on talking to someone when I have these horrible, dark thoughts screaming in my ear, relentlessly? I can't listen to you, because you'll never be able to talk louder, or more frantically, or more convincingly than the darkness.

Once my mom really saw how bad it was in person, she wanted to tell everything to the Rangers' sports psychologist, who was staying at the same hotel as we were. I couldn't take the shame and embarrassment of it all. I couldn't let go of my dream. I begged her not to tell him, so she grudgingly agreed. She tried to keep me distracted, so we did a bunch of touristy things in New York. Mom had never been to the city before, so we went to the Empire State Building and rode the elevator up to the top floor. The observation deck at the top of the Empire State Building is one of the most breathtaking views in the entire world. It's a 360-degree view from 102 stories above the Big Apple. It's the stuff of movies.

So you have to imagine—I'm there in this incredible place with my mom, who I love more than anything, and I'm about to watch my team play for a Stanley Cup, and even then I couldn't get out of the darkness. I couldn't enjoy the moment for a millisecond. All I could feel was pain. I was an empty husk of a human being.

I think we all have that moment in our life that will be a scar on our soul forever. Something that reminds us of what pain really means. For me, it's what happened at the top of the Empire State Building that day.

The observation deck has these tall wrought-iron fences all

around it—10 feet high. All of Manhattan is beneath you. You're living inside the postcard. It should give you goosebumps. But I just stared out at the skyscrapers, blank. They looked like Legos. I remember I leaned up against the fence like it was a cage, and I looked down at the streets below with this intense loneliness. Just total, bottomless despair. And then I turned and looked my mom right in the eyes and said:

"I wish I could jump."

All I wanted to do was die. An Olympic hero, a hockey star, and it didn't matter. Deep down, I thought I was a maniac. I thought that I would never have peace again. I didn't want to live anymore.

Mom started sobbing. And I could see in her face that she was thinking, *My God, how on earth did my baby boy get to this place?*

2

Why are people the way they are? Why do our lives turn out the way they do? I guess every story has an opening scene. Something that happens when we're kids that makes this puzzle of our lives make some kind of sense.

For me, it was probably when my mom caught the french fry. She's such a funny lady. We were sitting around in the kitchen one day, having burgers or hot dogs or something, and me being the wild little kid that I was, I chucked a french fry at her as a joke.

She flashed her left hand and snatched it clean out of the air. Me and my brother just looked at her in amazement. It was a perfect glove save. Sometimes you have to wonder if our destiny is somewhere deep in our DNA. *The Karate Kid* had just come out, so after that day, she became known around the house as Mr. Miyagi. What can I say? I grew up in Calgary, Alberta. We had to entertain ourselves.

I had two defining characteristics as a kid: my red hair and my passion for hockey. To be candid, I despised being a redhead when I was growing up. I got teased for it all the time, and I always felt that having red hair made me unattractive. Guys on my brother's hockey team called me "basketball head." At that age, even a stupid nickname like that marks you.

My parents were working-class, salt-of-the-earth people. Maybe it's a Canadian cliché, but sometimes the clichés are true. Dad was born in Prelate, Saskatchewan, and grew up with three brothers and two sisters in a two-bedroom farmhouse. It was a simple existence. As a teenager, my dad began working on the railroad for Canadian Pacific as a switchman, but later on he ended up becoming a plumber in the construction industry, where he spent the next 40 years. Dad worked on new builds. After houses were framed, he would do the plumbing. Imagine that job in the dead of winter in Calgary?

We're talking minus-20, minus-30, and the only thing between my dad and the frigid cold was some plywood. I respect my father so much for his resilience and drive. Come to think of it, that is likely where I got mine. He's a goddamned warrior in my eyes. He did what he had to do for his kids, going to work and slugging it out every day. He was your typical stoic father figure that that generation produced, but never have I questioned his love for me.

But I also have no doubt in my mind he could have used help with his own mental health growing up. As a kid, he slept with his three brothers in a tiny attic, and when he lost his two front teeth, the family didn't have the money to ever get them replaced. That's just the way it was back then. Imagine—my dad in a new high school, moving from a tiny town called Prelate in Saskatchewan to Medicine Hat, Alberta, with no front teeth and trying to make new friends. I feel for him. There are still things from his childhood that he refuses to discuss, but I know they were traumatizing. I can only imagine. Help back then was only for "crazy" people, and if a person was suffering, they suffered alone.

Ironically, it would be a preview of what was to come in my own life. Sometimes I wonder if trauma is baked into our DNA. Like how my mom catching that french fry was a preview of my destiny as a goalie, I wonder if my destiny to struggle with mental health issues was linked to my family's history.

My mom's father, Edward, had served in the Second World War. I idolized him. He was the most gentle soul I'd ever known, and I wanted to be just like him. He was so courageous and so kind. A rare combination. One day, I asked him why he had enlisted in the army during a World War, thinking, *Who in their right mind would want to go get shot at?*

In his kind and gentle way, he simply said to me, "Because that's just what we did." It was so matter-of-fact, and so honest. He rarely spoke about the war. I only heard the stories years after my grandpa's death. In one instance, he was sitting beside his best friend, bullshitting like guys would do in a hockey locker room, and his friend was cleaning his gun. The gun accidentally discharged, and my grandfather's friend shot himself in the head. It killed him instantly. I can't even imagine how much that probably scarred him. Where does anyone even begin to recover from that kind of trauma? What would that do to a person's mental health? I had heard that for years that after he came back from the war, he had nightmares and flashbacks. I'm no doctor, but that sounds like severe Post-Traumatic Stress Disorder (PTSD) to me. But of course, therapy for that genera-tion was almost non-existent. A person suffered in silence.

My grandma, on the other hand, was a tough woman. I don't recall a lot of warmth and kindness from her growing up. I never thought that she liked me, but the truth is, I'm pretty sure she wasn't happy with her own life. She smoked and drank like a rock star. I don't know, maybe having three kids, the first at age 18, and then becoming a grandma at 36, will do that to a person. My mom faced a lot of emotional abuse from her mother when she was growing up. She said it was never phys-ical. It was more mental, and it chipped away at my mom's self-esteem so badly.

So that's my foundation. I love my family, but I can see the lineage of emotional scars that run deep within our family tree. And it didn't just affect me, but affected my brother, Stacey, as well. He's four and a half years older than me. We were super close when we were little, but when he was a teenager, everything changed. One random winter morning, he stepped out the front door and onto the cement steps and slipped on some ice. He fell backwards violently and broke two vertebrae in his back. Mom took him to the doctor to get checked out, and the doctor prescribed him the painkiller Percocet.

And I think we've all seen this story play out too many times to count now. But this was the '80s, and painkillers were taken like candy. We barely thought anything of it. We were told they were completely harmless. Unfortunately for my brother, that prescription for Percocet ended up turning into a serious addiction to painkillers. And as the world now knows, once a person is addicted, those pills are as hard to get off as heroin.

After that, our relationship completely changed. He spent most of his time alone in his room. During that era, that kind of behaviour was mostly written off as "just being a surly teenager." Stacey was exhibiting all the classic signs of a serious mental health issue, but my parents' generation was not educated on mental health and had no idea what to do about it. Over time, I lost my brother. We became like strangers in our own house. And that still breaks my heart, and I'm sure that it shaped my life more than I even know.

And then there was me. Corey Hirsch.

Who the hell was I?

Well, looking back on it now, with all the wisdom we have today, I was an anxious kid who most likely had undiagnosed Attention Deficit Hyperactivity Disorder (ADHD). Back then, parents just shrugged and said, "Oh, he's just *hyperactive*." I couldn't sit still for more than a minute, and my anxiety, which was mistaken for curiosity, would usually get the best of me. I'm not even sure the terminology for ADHD even existed back then, but let's just say that I got *into things*. I was fascinated by anything mechanical, like record players, and I couldn't stop myself from breaking things just to see what was going on under all that plastic. My reputation started to precede me around the neighbourhood as a bit of a Dennis the Menace–type character, and all of a sudden I wasn't allowed to go back to certain people's houses.

My mom tells a great story about me going to the dentist when I was little. She says I was around four years old, and we were leaving his office, and there was a flight of stairs and the railings going down were just the perfect spacing for a hyperactive, curious little boy to stick his head through—you know, *just to see what will happen.*

Which, of course, I did. And of course I got my head stuck. My mom panicked and tried to pull me out. But I was crying and screaming so hard that my head swelled up even more. The harder she pulled, the more my head swelled. So then she started breaking down in a complete panic, and by now everyone in the office building had come out to see what the chaos was all about. This being Canada, she was totally horrified to imagine what those people were thinking about her. She thought for sure they were going to call the authorities to have me taken away for neglect.

My mom literally heard someone yell, "Call the fire department!!!!!" like they do in the movies. Hell, if I was her, I would have just wanted a shot of whiskey. After 15 minutes of hysteria, I guess I relaxed enough for my head to swell down to the proper size, and she finally succeeded in getting me free. Mom was so embarrassed, she couldn't get us out of there fast enough. We got into the car and she was a mess—makeup running down her face, her eyes swollen and puffy. And there was me in the back seat, grinning from ear to ear like nothing happened. Dennis the fucking Menace.

I'm sure she could have killed me. Anyway, our little journey wasn't over. Mom had to collect herself because we still had to go to the bank to deposit a cheque. You know where this is going, don't you? What did they have up at the teller's station at the bank back in the good old days? Come on, channel your inner child. You remember. That little gate with the shiny gold bars! Oh, yes. Mom was looking for her chequebook, and then she looked down at me and saw my eyes light up. I immediately started running over to those shiny gold bars. I made a break for it. I had to see what would happen. I was just about to stick my head through the bars again when Mom quickly grabbed my arm and said, "Don't even think about it!"

What can I say? I was, uh . . . well, let's say I was a *character*.

My mom swears that I used to sleep with one eye open as a

baby. What do you do with a kid like that? Easy. You put him in skates and let him go.

When I was around four, we moved to an area in Calgary called Forest Lawn and lived in a duplex that I vaguely remember. It was there where I first learned to skate. There was an outdoor community rink near our house, and Mom and Dad would put our skates on for us and lace 'em up. Mom says my ankles practically touched the ice as I tried skating for the first time, but I did it. Basically from that day on, I slept, ate, lived and breathed hockey. I would watch *Hockey Night in Canada* with my dad every Saturday night. For us, it was like going to church. Saturday night at six o'clock, we were in front of that TV, watching the Toronto Maple Leafs or, occasionally, the Montreal Canadiens. Those were the only hockey games on TV in Calgary at that time, since the Calgary Flames did not exist until 1980, when they moved from Atlanta.

Dad would take plumbing jobs on the side for a little extra money so he could take us to Calgary Cowboys games. The Cowboys played in the World Hockey Association. Right from the start, I was obsessed with goalies. "Smokey" McLeod was the starting goalie for the Cowboys, and he had a white mask with a red cowboy hat painted on the front. I was completely entranced by it. A person could be whatever character they wanted to be behind that mask. Smokey was his own character. He was a huge influence in my becoming a goalie. And by the way, in case you were wondering, he was called Smokey because he was a chain-smoker and would have a dart or two between periods. These were the days of "a smoke and a Coke" as intermission refreshment. Different times, indeed.

At home, we were huge Lanny McDonald fans, but my absolute favourite NHL player was Mike Palmateer of the Toronto Maple Leafs. It was his passion and how hard he worked that drew me in. He was so acrobatic. He did anything he could to stop the puck and be there for his teammates. That's why we all idolized him. When I was little, my mom would come into my room late at night whenever I wouldn't fall asleep, and we had this little ritual. She would pretend to pick up a phone and dial Mike Palmateer's mom. She would really sell it, like, "Hi, Mrs. Palmateer? Yes, it's Mrs. Hirsch. Can Mike come to the phone and talk to Corey? Okay, great."

Then she would hand me the pretend phone, and I would talk to Mike.

That was my mom in a nutshell.

We quickly became a hockey family. My brother had been signed up to play hockey, and I went to all his games. I became a rink rat. To me, finding an old puck that had gone over the glass and got stuck under the mouldy bleachers was like finding gold. Either you understand exactly what I mean, or you're shaking your head. But to me, hockey was an obsession. It was my happy place.

I was six years old when my dad first registered me for organized hockey. I went to my first practice and saw the goalie equipment in a plastic bag in the corner. The community actually supplied the goalie equipment, since it was so expensive for most families, and I begged my dad to ask the coach if I could take it. He refused, likely because he didn't want me to be a goalie—I mean, what parent wants their kid to have that kind of pressure? Dad told me if that I wanted to play goalie, I would have to ask the coach myself. As a six-year-old, I somehow mustered up the courage and staked my claim to the goalie gear. I never played any other position from that day forward.

In my second year of organized hockey, I don't really know how it was arranged, but our hockey team went to Los Angeles and played three or four teams there. We played two periods of hockey in the Great Western Forum, where the LA Kings played, and later that night, I saw my very first NHL game in person. It was March 1980, and we watched the Los Angeles Kings versus the Hartford Whalers. It was the height of the Kings' Triple Crown Line era with Marcel Dionne, Charlie Simmer and Dave Taylor. It was also Gordie Howe's final NHL season, and he was playing with Hartford. Everybody was crowding around Gordie after the game, but I had no idea who he was. I was only seven.

When I was on the ice, everything was comfortable. Everything was pure. Everything made sense. Off the ice, though, my life was changing. It's funny how these little butterfly-effect moments can change your course. When I was eight years old, the teachers in the public school system in Calgary went on strike. We weren't particularly religious, but my mom and dad decided that they didn't want me or my brother to miss any of our education, so they transferred us into a Catholic school. It quickly became apparent that life would be very different for me in that environment.

In fact, I think it was probably the earliest sign that I was going to have some serious issues with obsessive thoughts and anxiety. Religion class was mandatory, and I was not allowed to take communion or go to confession with the other kids, since I was yet to be baptized Catholic. When the time came for everybody to see the priest and go to confession, I sat in the hall by myself as each of my classmates went in. The concept of sinning and everlasting hell was introduced to me, and those can be pretty heavy thoughts for a child to wrap their mind around, especially if they're seeing themselves as an outsider. That's when my wheels really started turning for the first time, and I kind of fell down into a dark hole.

There were nights during my Catholic school days that I couldn't sleep. I would lie there going through my day, wondering whether I had done anything wrong, and whether the "offence" was a ticket straight to hell. If you want a little taste of what it feels like to deal with obsessive thoughts, just close your eyes and meditate on the concept of infinity and hell for a few minutes. Watch how fast you panic and try to think about *any-thing* else. Then imagine you can't. It's very possible that was the beginning of my obsessive worrying. I don't blame the Catholic church or the school at all, but I do think that it was the first trigger for me of guilt, anxiety and the loop that my brain can fall into.

As a kid, my refuge was always sports. I was just always good at anything athletic. Put a football or hockey stick in my hand, and I can play and be natural at it. Anything athletic makes sense to me. School was the opposite. With my undiagnosed ADHD and being teased mercilessly for being a redhead, I felt ugly and dumb at school, which chipped away at my self-esteem. So it's natural that sports became my identity, because that's where people liked me.

I had a teacher in sixth grade who saw how I struggled with schoolwork but dominated anything athletic. I think he thought I was a show-off, a kid who put little effort into books but had some crazy pipe dream of playing in the NHL. I remember when he flat-out told me to my face, when I was 11, that I would never play in the NHL. He said it was such a long shot that I should stop wasting my time dreaming of it and get serious. I couldn't believe he said that. My mom was pissed! She went down to my elementary school and gave this teacher an absolute verbal beating. I guess it must have worked, because I never heard about it from that teacher again.

The infinitesimal odds of making the NHL are not in a kid's favour, but why crush their dreams? My mentality was *Hey, somebody's gotta make it.* There are more than 750 guys playing in the NHL, and every one of them knew the odds. A child should be advised to get an education, but why can't they have both? Let a child dream big, enjoy the game for what it is and for the life lessons it teaches. It's a great game.

Fortunately, I had some great mentors along the way. My parents would scrape up a little extra money during the summers to send me to Medicine Hat Tigers Hockey Schools. (I mean, what a name, eh?) As luck would have it, Kelly Hrudey, who was a budding NHL superstar goaltender, was one of the goaltending coaches there. That's where I really learned to play goal. Life has so many crazy twists and turns. I just happened to get taught by one of the best goalies to ever play in the NHL at a little hockey school in a small town of 65,000 people. Luck and timing definitely helped.

When I was 12, the New York Islanders came to town, and my dad found out where the team was staying in Calgary. I don't know what possessed my dad to do this, but he called up Kelly Hrudey at the hotel! Again, different times! You could do that back then. He just told the guy at the desk to connect him to Mr. Hrudey's room, and he did it. Kelly actually picked up the phone, and my dad invited him to have a coffee with us. My father literally pulled me out of school, and we went downtown to meet Kelly. Man, I was so excited. It was the best surprise ever. It was on a game day, for God's sake, and Kelly took the time to see us. What NHLer would do that out of the blue for some kid? Kelly even gave me one of his goalie sticks. He showed me how a true NHL professional and gentleman acts. What a guy. You need people like that to show you that your dreams are worth fighting for, and how to act when you get there.

By the time I was 15, I was being looked at as a top prospect in juniors. I made the Calgary Canucks Junior A team as a

15-year-old—almost unheard of for a goalie. I was playing with 20-year-olds and really excelling. I was still going to high school and living at home, of course, and I was too young to drive. So I actually took the C-Train and a bus to practice every day while the other players drove. Some of my teammates went to college and others even had day jobs. What an incredible team we had. We set a league record by winning 21 consecutive games and finished first overall in the AJHL that season.

Our team made it all the way to the Western Canada final for the Abbott Cup, where we matched up in a seven-game series versus the Saskatchewan Junior Hockey League champions, the Notre Dame Hounds. The winner of that series would go on to the national championship. On that Notre Dame team were future NHL stars Rod Brind'Amour and goaltender Curtis Joseph (the legendary "Cujo"). They beat us in a thrilling Game 7 finale in which I started as a 15-year-old against a 20-year-old Cujo down at the other end. We lost, but I knew that I had made my mark.

That season was meaningful for another reason, too. It was dedicated to our fallen teammate, an 18-year-old kid named

Kraig Thorson. It was the first time I experienced how cruel cancer can be. Thor was in remission from cancer treatment when he made the team out of training camp. He played a few months with us, but just before Christmas, he stopped coming to the rink for games or practice. We were told his cancer had returned. I never thought much of it, thinking he'd get better and be back in no time, but we didn't see him much after that. He came to one practice after his cancer came back, desperately wanting to get better and play again.

I remember seeing him sitting on a chair in the locker room, tying his skates, slumped over. He looked so frail and weak—not even close to the guy who made our team. He could barely tie them up. I went out on the ice early with him and had him take a few shots on me. He couldn't lift the puck, but he wanted to be out there more than anything. He helped out the rest of practice by shuffling some pucks, cracked a few jokes in the locker room, changed and went home.

A few months passed, and we hadn't seen him back at the rink. I was getting on the bus to go to a road game in February of 1988. I sat in my seat and I looked around. It was eerily silent. Dean Larson, one of our top players, had a tear rolling down his cheek. And that's when it hit me. Thor was gone. He was only 18.

I still have that vivid memory of him tying up his skates in the locker room. He was in so much pain, but he just wanted to be out there on the ice. He wanted to hear that first little *crunch* underneath his feet. He wanted to be out there where he could feel free. Where everything made sense. I think every hockey player can relate to that feeling. I know I can. It probably saved my life.

3

There were always little signs of the darkness.

I was 17 years old the first time I considered taking my life. And it was over the dumbest thing imaginable. I was ready to throw everything away, all because I was passed over in the 1990 NHL Draft. The worst part is that it wasn't even my last chance. It was just the first draft that I was eligible for. I could still stay in juniors and try again next year. But I took it so hard, because my entire identity was tied to my success as a hockey player.

When my name didn't get called, I was just so embarrassed, and embarrassment is pure poison for someone with mental health issues. I felt ashamed because I was slated to be drafted throughout most of that season, and some reports even suggested that I'd go early. I was playing for the Kamloops Blazers of the Western Hockey League under Ken Hitchcock, and despite living all on my own a long way from home, and despite the 15-hour bus rides from British Columbia to Regina or Manitoba or wherever the heck we were playing that week, I was really coming into my own as a goalie and as a person. I fought through the homesickness and really bonded with some of the older players, and Hitch was phenomenal to me. We hear so many horror stories about bullying and abuse in junior hockey these days, but I was really lucky and I never experienced any of that in Kamloops. It was a tremendous group of guys.

And we were so good. My God, were we good. It's every goalie's dream to play with a guy like Scott Niedermayer, who was new to our team and just 16. It's ridiculous how good he was even at that age. He took over games on his own. Niedermayer was the best player I ever played with, in fact. Just pure skill and poise. That whole season had gone great. We won the

Western Hockey League championship, and I could basically taste my NHL dream. But then I experienced what every goalie fears in the back of their mind. I experienced a total collapse in a big moment.

After coasting along for most of my hockey career, I got lit up at the Memorial Cup. I could feel my game coming apart, and I didn't know how to pull it back together. We lost the opening game 8–7 in overtime to Kitchener, and then lost 7–6 in overtime to Oshawa. We were eliminated in the third game by Laval, losing 4–2.

I had allowed 19 goals in only three games. If you want to really feel naked, put on some goalie equipment and let up 19 goals in three games, when all of your buddies are counting on you. It's a goalie's worst nightmare. Obviously, my stock plummeted. My confidence was dinged. Teams wanted to make sure I wasn't a "head case" who lost it in the big moments. So I got passed over at the '90 draft.

It was so devastating to me, because it didn't feel like they passed on Corey Hirsch the hockey player. It felt like they passed on *Corey Hirsch*. I could not separate the two things. My whole *being* was hockey. All my value. All my self-worth. I think a lot of people who throw themselves completely into their work—whether they are a lawyer or an entrepreneur or a teacher—can probably relate to what I'm saying. When things went wrong, they didn't go wrong "at work." They went wrong with *me*. I simply couldn't leave it all behind at the rink. If I played well, then I was a good person that day. If I played poorly, then I was not worthy of anything. I was garbage. A terrible goalie. A terrible human being. That's simply how my mind always worked.

Let up five goals in a game?

You're worthless. You're complete shit. You're shit, shit, shit. Why would anyone love you? Nobody even likes you, man. You're trash. A fraud. You always end up letting everyone down. That's the worst part. All your buddies were counting on you, and what did you do? You fucking blew it. You idiot. You know what? Everyone would be better if you weren't around. You should just kill yourself.

That's how my brain would lie to me, on a loop, until I was able to go out again the next time and play well. If I had another bad game, it was another few days of utter despair and self-hatred. So when I didn't get drafted, I saw myself as a complete failure, and not just to myself but to my whole family and all my friends. In my warped brain, the only way to escape from the embarrassment seemed to be suicide. I just had no clue that what I was experiencing was not normal, and no knowledge of how to help myself. So I was bent on destruction.

That was the first time that I drove up to the top of the mountain in Kamloops and contemplated driving off the cliff. I sat there in my car, sobbing uncontrollably, wondering how I could go on. I think the only reason that I was able to keep going was that I still had another year to prove myself and reach my NHL dreams. It's sad, looking back, how much of my will to live was tied into my success as a hockey player. But that's just the way it was. After 30 minutes of staring into the abyss, I was able to gather myself and drive home. Unfortunately, I would return to that same cliff just four years later, in a much, much worse place.

You know, I often think about that classic quote from Bernie Parent about hockey goalies. You know the one. "You don't have to be crazy to be a goalie . . . but it *helps*."

I have a really complicated relationship with that cliché. My mental health struggles absolutely did not make me a better goalie. It was not a superpower. It was crippling. But I do think that there is a certain type of brain that is attracted to putting on the mask and protecting their team at all costs. And I use that word *protecting* very specifically. Despite everything that was going on in my brain off the ice, once I put on that mask and got into my net, it was like I was a different person.

You have to understand what it feels like to actually be a goalie. A lot of people think that you're just throwing yourself into shots. That you're reacting. "See puck, stop puck." In fact, it's a lot more cerebral than that, especially at higher levels.

For 60 minutes, all you are thinking about is danger. Danger, danger, danger. Threats everywhere that must be scanned. You must protect that net at all costs. You must protect your team at all costs. You don't hear the crowd. You don't hear the music playing on the PA. You don't think about anything that's going on in your life. The best way that I can describe it is that scene in *The Terminator* where they show the perspective through the Terminator's eyes. You know how the supercomputer screen is glowing in infrared, and he's constantly scanning his environment for new threats, and the machine is like *doot-doot-doot THREAT DETECTED*? That's what it's like inside a goalie's brain as the play is unfolding. You're not just tracking the puck and reacting to it. That's what you do in peewee hockey. At the higher levels, you learn to scan the whole ice like it's a chessboard. For hours, your brain is doing nothing but *assessing the danger*. Because even during time outs and before faceoffs, you're doing all the calculus and physics of dangerous scenarios in your head.

Defenceman is cheating in at the top of the circle. Wicked left-handed shot. If the centre wins it back clean, come out aggressive to cut down his angle. He'll want to shoot. But don't forget about the winger on the back side. And don't drop down too early. And don't forget about ...

It goes on and on like this in real time, endlessly, for the entire game. You're in a state of hyper-hyper-hyper-vigilance and almost a controlled paranoia.

Sure, on the surface, you are thinking: *Do not let that puck in that net.*

But there's something more frantic and telling going on.

Somewhere deep in your subconscious, you are really thinking: *Do not get embarrassed, do not get embarrassed, do not get embarrassed. There's 15,000 people watching you. All eyes on you. Do not lose the game. Do not lose your job. Do not lose your identity.*

The underlying anxiety fuels the vigilance. And I think that's why certain types of brains are drawn to playing goalie and throwing themselves in front of pucks. You're almost at home in all that chaos and fear and paranoia. But then what happens when you get off the ice? It's not so easy to shut down that Terminator supercomputer. You look for the plug to turn it off so you can go to sleep, and it's not there. It's always *on*. Scanning, worrying, searching for the next catastrophe. A lot of guys turn to alcohol and drugs to power it down. Especially when you're getting back to the hotel at one o'clock in the morning after a bad loss, or even after a great win, and your brain is still on fire, and the adrenalin is rushing through your body, and your head hits that pillow and you think: *NOPE.*

So a lot of goalies almost learn to live in a state of perpetual ON. A state of constant low-level anxiety and vigilance. That's why they call us "crazy." That's why we're often the guys and girls on the team who keep to ourselves and seem like we're off somewhere in our own little world. It can be a lonely place, but we learn to live in it, and even thrive in it. The consequences often come later on.

That's the best way I can describe how I was to make it all the way to the NHL in one of the highest-pressure jobs in sports despite being extremely, extremely sick. If I had a super-power, it wasn't my illness. It was my ability to be strong as hell in spite of it.

I came down off that mountain after the disappointment of the 1990 NHL Draft and put together another really solid season with Kamloops, but when the 1991 draft rolled around, even my agent, Don Meehan, told me that I should probably stay home and listen to it on the radio, because he still wasn't sure that I'd get taken. Failure in big moments can haunt goalies forever, no matter what happens the following season. Once you have "the stink" on you, it can be hard to get it off. I was bracing myself for another summer of disappointment and embarrassment.

I sat down in front of the radio when it started, and I waited.

And I waited and waited and waited and waited. The rounds started ticking by—fifth round, sixth round, seventh round— and I was starting to sweat. Then, all the way in the eighth round, I heard the Kamloops Blazers play-by-play announcer, Kelly Moore, say the magic words.

"With the 169th pick . . . the New York Rangers select . . . Corey Hirsch."

It was probably the single greatest moment of my life. Calling your mom and dad to tell them that you're going to the NHL . . . well, there's no words that can describe that feeling. All the memories come flooding back. The whole journey. You remember the first time seeing Smokey in his blood-red Cowboy mask. You remember your mom handing you the fake telephone so you could tell Mike Palmateer that he had a great game. You remember sitting on the floor and watching *Hockey Night in Canada* with your dad.

And then you realize: *Holy hell . . . That's really going to be* me *out there. I'm going to be on that TV. Some little kid is going to be looking at my mask and saying, "Whoa."*

At that moment, when I heard my name called by the Rangers, I really thought that the darkness and the pain and the anxiety was all over. That was all just stupid teenage angst. It was all just a big misunderstanding. A bad moment.

After all the doubt, I had finally achieved my dream. All my worries were for nothing. I was a good goalie. I was a good person. I was *worth* something. I was going to be a freaking New York Ranger. I was in heaven, man. Heaven.

I had no idea the hell that was awaiting me.

4

More signs. More little breadcrumbs of what was to come. The footsteps.

I couldn't get them out of my brain. It felt like they were slowly driving me insane. They were all that I could think about. They echoed constantly in my brain, like bombs going off every three seconds. They were so loud that I would crawl into the fetal position, trembling like a child.

This was the fall of 1992. I was 20 years old, playing for the Rangers' farm team in Binghamton, New York. My anxiety was through the roof, because I was in a new environment without any of my friends from juniors. I was playing with grown men who were competing to put food on the table for their families. I was thousands of miles from home. I was truly *alone*, for the first time in my life.

The Rangers kept me with the team until the end of training camp, so by the time I got to Binghamton, most guys had already been there for weeks. They'd had their living situations settled, and I had to find my own place. I rented a seedy apartment on the bottom floor of an old apartment complex. The only thing between me and the people above me was a thin plywood floor.

From the very first night I moved in, I could hear every step they took. Most people have been in that situation. It's so annoying, right? It's hard not to think about. You try to watch TV, and you hear the echo. After a couple minutes, it's still annoying, but you subconsciously tune it out, right? Well, my brain didn't process the noise like a "normal" person's brain. In my head, their steps were so loud that they sounded like fireworks going off. So loud that I felt actual pain. It was like every step they took was a sledgehammer to my temple.

Within days, I stopped sleeping. When the footsteps stopped, my brain would simply obsess over when they would begin again. It was like I was waiting for a bomb to go off. And then the panic attacks started. They were unrelenting. During the day, I would sit on my couch just staring at the ceiling, waiting for the noise to end. It got so bad that every day I would leave my apartment and drive aimlessly around town for hours. I would hope the people upstairs would be in bed by the time I got back and there would be silence. I couldn't understand why it was happening. Other players on the team lived in the same complex with people living above them, and it never bothered them. Why was it so loud to me? It sounded to me as if there were elephants walking above me. Why did it bother me so much and not them?

Noise sensitivity is a common symptom of ADHD, but I didn't even know that I had ADHD back then. I just thought that I was going insane. I would do anything to try and make the anxiety go away. I once turned on the shower and got in with all my clothes on. I was hoping to drown out the footsteps with the sound of the shower, but then I found myself at the bottom of my bathtub, crying uncontrollably. I was bawling, begging for the noise to stop or for someone to come get me and take me back home.

I finally moved apartments, and it didn't work. Footsteps. *Thud-thud. Thud-thud-thud. THUDTHUDTHUDTHUD IT'LL NEVER STOP IT'LL NEVER END NOISE NOISE NOISENOISENOISE.*

I moved again, and again, trying to find a place that was quiet, trying to run from my own brain. I lost $5,000 in security deposits that year, but I didn't care. I would have paid anything to get rid of the overwhelming anxiety, to make the obsession with the noise stop. I wanted to go home so badly, but there was no way I could. It would have ruined any shot I had at playing in the NHL. I had to stay and suffer through the crippling anxiety in silence.

The strangest part of it all was that I was having an amazing season on the ice. The rink was the only place where I felt peace. The minute I stepped on that ice, everything got quiet. But literally the minute I stepped off the ice and took off my mask, my brain was on fire again. I was already thinking about the noise that awaited me at home. So sometimes I would just drive around after the game for hours, until three in the morning, staring at the lines in the road.

I would often call Bob Froese, my goalie coach, and try to hold back the tears. I told him I was lonely and struggling, but I didn't fully explain what was happening in my brain. I was reaching out for help, the best way that I could. Bob was like a father figure to me, someone I trusted completely. He wanted to help me, but I don't think he ever knew the extent of what I was going through. Nobody did. It was just so taboo to admit that things weren't right inside your head. Bob always did his best to be a friend and coach, but what I really needed was a therapist.

I was so lonely. The anxiety and panic attacks were all I could handle. I could finally see light at the end of the tunnel after Christmas. I moved once more—the fifth time that season—finding a top-floor apartment. With no one living above me, there was no noise to trigger my anxiety, and I started to come around. I have no idea how, but I was having a record-breaking year.

Off the ice, I was a wreck.

On the ice, my record was 19–2–3. I led the AHL in all statistical categories.

That's the extent to which I could compartmentalize my brain.

One night, Bob was sitting in my apartment with me, watching the Rangers play on TV, when my phone rang. It was my dad. My grandpa on my father's side, Kasper, had been killed in a head-on car accident. I hung up the phone and sat down beside Bob, in shock. I didn't know this grandpa as well as my mom's father, but he was kind and a good man. He once drove 12 hours to watch me play in Kamloops, stayed in a hotel for two nights and gave me a crisp new $50 bill when he left. I know he didn't have a penny to his name, but he still gave me $50.

The news of his death was heartbreaking. Bob sat with me in silence for a minute and didn't know what to say. He knew that the Rangers were about to call me up to the team for my first NHL game, but he wasn't supposed to let me know until it was finalized. He broke the rules and told me, and asked me what I wanted to do. The plan was for me was to meet the team in Montreal in the coming days, which would conflict with the funeral.

I called my dad, and we talked about what my grandpa would want. He eased my mind and told me to stay with the team, because my grandpa would have wanted me to live out my dream more than anything in the world. I met the team in Montreal the next night, and I backed up John Vanbiesbrouck at the old Montreal Forum. The next day, we flew to Detroit, and I was told my first start would be against the Red Wings at the famous Joe Louis Arena.

The Red Wings had some incredible players—Steve Yzerman, Sergei Fedorov, Dino Ciccarelli, Ray Sheppard. Every skater remembers their first goal as an NHL player and who they scored it on. There's a tradition that they get to keep the puck and it goes on a plaque. Goalies, on the other hand, always remember the first guy who scored on them. For me, it was Jimmy Carson. He blew the puck by me. I didn't even move, and I definitely didn't get a plaque. Sheldon Kennedy scored the second goal on me that night. But I was able to remain calm, and the game ended in a 2–2 tie. I was even selected as one of the Three Stars of the game. I knew my grandpa was looking down on me, and that he was very proud.

After my first NHL start, we stayed overnight in Detroit. The guys took me out for a beer to celebrate. Sheldon Kennedy happened to be at the same bar that we had picked. Four or five of my teammates were sitting with me, and we saw Sheldon at the end of the bar, surrounded by a few people. One of my teammates noticed him and said, "Hey, Hirschey, stay away from that guy. He's bad news." Sheldon was drinking a lot and didn't have a good reputation off the ice. His teammates loved him, though, and at the rink he was an amazing player.

Of course, there was a very good reason for the darkness. There always is.

In December 1986, while he was playing with the Swift Current Broncos of the Western Hockey League, he was a passenger in the tragic bus crash that killed four of his teammates. He and the remaining survivors were denied any form of grief therapy by their coach, Graham James. Sheldon was being sexually abused by that same coach. James ended up serving time in prison for his crimes after other players came forward with their stories of abuse. Sheldon was self-medicating for his horrific trauma, and instead of receiving help, he was simply labelled as a "bad guy" around the league.

It just goes to show you that you never know what's going on underneath the surface, even with people you assume are operating at a high level.

Four nights later, since I had played so well versus Detroit, I was told, I would get the start against the Los Angeles Kings at the LA Forum, the very same place I played as a seven-year-old and watched Gordie Howe play. The Kings were loaded, with Wayne Gretzky, Jari Kurri and Paul Coffey, just to name a few. I was hoping that my idol Kelly Hrudey would be in net for them, but unfortunately he didn't get the start.

That night, I started out well. I didn't allow any goals in the first period. I was feeling good, but just as things were rolling along in the second period, the Kings torched me for three goals in a row. The period ended, and my brain started to fire anxious thoughts at me right away. Usually, during a game, I could stay pretty focused. But this was the NHL. This was Gretzky and the Kings. This was my whole livelihood hanging in the balance. If I melted down in my second NHL start, who knew what could happen? *Wait, what if I just kept letting in goals? What*

if it was 5–0? 7–0? 13–0? What if I never stopped another shot?
Everyone in the arena is looking at you. Your teammates are looking
at you. All eyes on you. All eyes, all eyes, all eyes. You're failing, you're
failing, you're failing. The puck is small. It's so small. It's coming so
fast. You're failingfailingfailingfailingfailing.

When we got to the locker room, my equipment felt really tight. Like it was suffocating me. I felt trapped. I felt a panic attack coming on.

I had to do something quickly, so I stripped off all my gear, got completely undressed, and jumped in the shower. During intermission, this is unheard of. You only have 15 minutes! I could feel the guys looking at me, like, "What in the hell is this kid *doing?*" Remember, I'm not a vet. This is my second game. Nobody said anything, and I was hoping they would write it off as just another goalie being weird. I towelled off, got dressed in a flash and went out for the third period.

Dove should have given me an endorsement deal. The shower worked. I went out there and shut Gretzky and the Kings down the rest of the way. I got my first NHL win, 8–3, after suffering a panic attack.

With the shower, it was almost like I hit the reset button on my brain. I don't know why, but the water felt cleansing. All through my whole career, I did that ritualistic behaviour when something bad happened on the ice. Sometimes, it would simply be to take off my pads and then put them back on again. Other times, I took a full shower, depending on how bad my anxiety was. After a while, guys wouldn't even bat an eye. It was just, "Oh, there goes Hirschey."

After my two weeks in the big time, I got sent back to Binghamton. Naively, every day for the rest of the year, I waited for the Rangers to trade a goalie so I could get called back up again. It never happened. Late in the season, with the Rangers out of the playoffs, I finally got that call.

I probably should have let it ring!

Because on the other end of the line was an invitation to meet Mr. Mario Lemieux for the very first time. We were playing the juggernaut Penguins, and the Rangers wanted me in the net.

(Spoiler alert: It did not go well.)

April 9, 1993. Madison Square Garden. Hoo boy.

You have to understand that Penguins team. They were

absolutely stacked. They had Mario, sure, but also Jaromir Jagr, Ron Francis, Kevin Stevens and Rick Tocchet. They had won 15 games in a row coming into MSG, and boy were they ever ready to add to that total. Sometimes you just know you're about to get run out of the building. You can feel it in the air, right from warmups.

It was a beating from the opening faceoff. No amount of showers was going to help me. I had already been torched for four goals when Mario got a breakaway on me in the second period. There's greatness, and then there's *greatness*. Gretzky and Mario were just in a different world. He came right down the centre of the ice with speed, made a couple of sick moves, and I bit so hard. He went one way and I went the other. Mario had an ocean of net to put the puck in. It was ridiculous, and very much worth looking up on YouTube if you want a laugh.

Honestly, I was so out of position that Mario could have skated back to the bench and grabbed a golf putter to tap it in. Watching the video replay of it the next day, I could literally see guys trying to get off the ice and onto the bench while Mario collected the puck at centre ice just so they wouldn't get a minus on the stat sheet. I got mercifully pulled after two periods with the score 5–3. The final score ended up 10–4 for Pittsburgh.

At the final buzzer, the whole crowd at Madison Square Garden gave Mario a standing ovation.

Dejected and beaten, I was sent back to the minors in Binghamton for the last few weeks of the season. By that time, I was mentally drained, physically exhausted from the lack of sleep and beaten down by my own brain. I had to find a way to get out of Binghamton, because the place was so deeply associated with anxiety and depression for me. It felt like a black hole. Unfortunately, I was stuck. I hadn't proved enough for the Rangers to call me up full time. I was going to be down in Binghamton for another season at least. It filled me with dread and hopelessness.

And that's when I got another lucky break that probably saved my life yet again.

It was a one-in-a-million stroke of luck and timing. The International Olympic Committee wanted to stagger the Winter and Summer Games, and that meant a Winter Games in 1992, then again in 1994. And guess who was chosen to be the coach of Team Canada for the '94 Olympics? Tom Renney, who had been my junior coach in Kamloops. He wanted me on the team.

The timing was perfect.

The Rangers thought that it would be great for my development, and they brokered a deal to let me leave the farm team and join Team Canada for the entire 1993–94 hockey season. I was going to get the chance to represent my country in Lillehammer. But before that, we were going to travel the world playing exhibition games. It not only got me out of the endless rut that I was in, but it kept me moving. It gave me some new faces and new places to see. It was like a stay of execution.

It was so much fun that it felt like being a kid again. It was, quite literally, the time of my fucking life. Even if it did end up with me on a Swedish postage stamp.

5

In order for you to understand how fun it was playing for Team Canada back in the days before cellphones and Twitter, I have to tell you a quick prank story.

Canada's Olympic roster was composed of a potpourri of players. There were NHL veterans such as Chris Kontos, and a number of players who were very good but not yet household names, like Adrian Aucoin. But then when Petr Nedved and Paul Kariya joined us, we became a different team. Nedved joined us after Christmas, but because he was originally from the Czech Republic, we wondered how he was going to get his Canadian citizenship in time. Somehow, they got it done. Kariya, who also joined us after Christmas, was a college player and had to finish his first semester at the University of Maine.

That season was the most fun I ever had playing hockey. I was newly single, and I actually got to live at home with my parents in Calgary, since that was where the National Team was based. I was happy, comfortable and stable. It was like a brief and amazing calm in the storm of my brain.

The team consisted of 23 guys, most of whom were also single and between the ages of 19 and 25. We travelled the world playing hockey. How could it get any better? I played 45 games that year, and won 24, lost 17 and tied 3.

We had a lot of fun along the way. Chris Kontos was one of the older guys on the team. He had already played eight seasons in the NHL. He was quite a prankster, too. I don't know how he even came up with this stuff—but somehow he had a suitcase full of wigs and false teeth made up for himself, and at a pre-Olympic tournament in Sweden, he put them to use. He convinced one of the security guards to let him borrow his jacket and cap. Chris put those on, along with a pair of glasses, and tucked the set of phony teeth in his mouth. Pretending to be Olympic security, he woke up Tom Renney and Dany Dubé, our coaches, and told them he had to talk to Paul Kariya at the security desk right away. Tom and Dany went and got Paul.

That's when the big "security guard" took them all to an interrogation room and started grilling Paul with a bunch of phony questions about who knows what—drugs, passports, girls, whatever. It got really heated. Tom Renney was ready to fight the security guard when all of a sudden he started cracking up. Kontos pulled off the hat, took off the glasses and spat out the goofy teeth.

"You're all under arrest by order of the Swedish Olympic Authority!!!!"

It was hilarious—we got a bag-skate the next day, but it was worth it. That was my pre-Olympics experience in a nutshell. It was like playing youth hockey with all your buddies.

The Olympic Games themselves were played in Lillehammer, a small town of less than 25,000 in the middle of Norway. It was stunning and picturesque. Because the town was so small for such a large international event, many of those who lived in Lillehammer worked on the event in some capacity, volunteering as drivers or security or whatever. Every family member who travelled to Norway to support the Canadian team stayed in someone's actual home. It was like something straight out of the Hallmark Channel.

Believe it or not, we weren't the favourites. Not at all. I believe eighth place was the highest ranking we got from the media, and I didn't think we'd get past the heavily favoured USA team. My parents asked if they should come to the Games, but I told them it'd be better to stay home. The town was small, and I had no idea where they would stay. Plus, it would have cost a small fortune for them to go, and I didn't want them to spend that kind of money. I was glad they didn't go, only because I wasn't sure I could have focused as well. I would have worried about them the whole time.

The opening ceremony was incredible. Walking into the bowl of the ski jump where they held the opening ceremony with all these athletes from every country around the world was pure magic. I will say this, though—it was bloody freezing! The coldest cold I've ever felt. It was minus-40 with the wind chill, and it was nighttime there. We were in this outrageous costume attire to look good on TV, and the clothing was paper-thin. We wore these winter jackets draped with Superman-style capes and trapper hats. On our feet we had these Santa Claus–style black boots that were made of thin felt and had rubber toes. It looked great on TV, but any longer in the elements and we were all going to die of exposure.

The plan for the big finale of the opening ceremony was for a ski jumper to jump off the ramp with the lit torch and then hand the torch to another person, who would walk it up the steps of the stadium and light the Olympic cauldron. The rumour was that the day before in rehearsal, the ski jumper who was supposed to jump had crashed really bad and hurt himself. They had to replace him with another amateur jumper. I could tell the guy was nervous as hell. Watching from the stands, I was nervous *for* him. Thankfully, he landed his jump and handed off the torch. The person he handed it to ran up the steps, stood beside the cauldron and paused for what seemed like an eternity. We were all freezing, and I don't know who it was, but another athlete sitting in front of me screamed out, "Just *light* the fucking thing already!"

The whole section burst out in laughter. Goddamn, it was cold. Goddamn, what a great memory.

Lillehammer was just incredible. It was so cool to see all the athletes from around the world in different sports. We stayed in the Athletes' Village with a 24-hour buffet-style cafeteria. Going for meals, I'd see athletes like Alberto Tomba, the Italian alpine ski champion, and tons of other cool people. But if you remember Lillehammer, you probably remember it for something very different: the Tonya Harding–Nancy Kerrigan figure skating scandal. (For all the kids out there, Tonya Harding's boyfriend clubbed her rival Nancy Kerrigan on the leg right before the Olympics. It dominated the news cycle.)

Once we got onto the ice, I was starting to feel as though I was heating up. I played well against Italy and we won 7–2. We then beat France 3–1 in our second game, and that set up Game 3 of the round-robin against our rivals, Team USA. They had beaten us eight times in 11 games leading up to the Olympics, but for most of those, we didn't have Kariya or Nedved. We dominated most of that game and were up 3–2 late when they scored to tie it. The game ended in a 3–3 tie. The next game, we lost our only game in the round-robin to Hall of Fame player Peter Stastny and the Slovakians, dropping a 3–1 decision. In our final game of the round-robin, we finished with a 3–2 win over Sweden. They were considered one of the favourites to win the gold, so that gave our team a lot of confidence.

With the round-robin portion over, it was on to a one-game elimination. Lose and you're done. In the quarter-final, a terrible penalty called on the Czech Republic in overtime helped us beat them 3–2, with Kariya scoring in OT. Manny Legace was so excited when we scored that he tried to jump over the boards, but with all his goalie equipment weighing him down, his leg got caught and he landed on his head. He wasn't hurt, but we must have watched the replay 20 times the next day, laughing our asses off.

We survived the first round and made it to the semis. Nobody expected us to finish higher than eighth, and here we were in the top four. We ended up playing our best game of the season against Saku Koivu and Finland in the semifinal. The Finns had dominated everyone at the tournament and destroyed the USA in the quarter-final 6–1. In an odd coaching decision,

Finland started their backup goalie against us. It seemed like they thought they would breeze through our team and wanted to rest their starter for the final. Big mistake. We were down 2–0 early, but we scored five unanswered goals in 30 minutes. The game ended 5–3. It was unbelievable. We had earned a spot in the gold medal game.

As I sat on the bus after the game, it hit me: win or lose, I was getting an Olympic medal. Corey Hirsch, from Calgary, Alberta, the kid who could barely function just a year before, was going to receive an Olympic medal. No matter what happened for the rest of my life, no one could ever take that away from me. I had a smile from ear to ear.

The final was on TV early Sunday morning back home. Hockey was the grand finale for the '94 Olympic Games, and neither team would disappoint. The goaltending matchup for that game was me versus Tommy Salo. Sweden got off to a quick start scoring in the first period on a power play. Peter Forsberg was behind the net and made a pass behind his back to Håkan Loob, who got the puck to the point, and Tomas Jonsson beat me with a one-timer. The rest of the game was mostly dominated by the Swedes, but with strong defensive play and good goaltending, we kept the game within striking distance at 1–0 until the third. Paul Kariya and Derek Mayer scored back-to-back on Tommy Salo in the third, and we led 2–1 late in the game. We were in control, and it looked like we would take the gold, when defenceman Brad Werenka got called for a marginal penalty late in the third period.

On the ensuing power play, Forsberg fed a pass to Magnus Svensson, and his point shot was headed wide, but it went off my defenceman's skate into the net. Tie game. With less than two minutes to go. It was heartbreaking.

We were going to overtime for the gold.

The play was fairly even in overtime, as neither team wanted to give an inch. We were deadlocked. With no winner, the game went to a shootout. Growing up in North America, we were at a clear disadvantage in shootouts. The European teams played their entire hockey lives with shootouts and practised them daily. I wasn't a very good breakaway goaltender. I was a stand-up-style goalie. Manny Legace, my backup, played more of a butterfly style and was an excellent breakaway goalie. There was a chance our coaches might have put him in for that shootout, but Manny had gotten injured when a puck hit him in the knee during warmup, and he was out of the game.

It was all down to me, with the world watching.

In his Hockey Canada track suit and crutches, Manny came down to the bench before the shootout. He called me over, leaned in and gave me a bit of advice, telling me to let the shooter make the first move—meaning *be patient*. That was exactly what Bob Froese would have said to me, and exactly what I needed to hear.

In the first round, Petr Nedved scored with a wicked wrist shot. We were up 1–0 to start. Then, in a surreal moment, I went nose to nose with Håkan Loob and stopped him cold. As a kid, I grew up watching him play for the Calgary Flames. Loob was one of my favourite players.

The second round started with Kariya scoring. We went up 2–0, and in my mind, there was no reason why we wouldn't win. I would do my part, and we just needed one more goal in our next three shots. However, in Sweden's second attempt, Magnus Svensson took me wide. I couldn't match his speed, and with me sprawling, he scored on an open net. We were still in control, though, ahead 2–1.

In round three, Dwayne Norris from Newfoundland took our third shot and was stopped, then Mats Näslund came down and tried to deke. He lost the puck on the chewed-up ice. The shootout remained at 2–1.

Next up, Tommy Salo stopped Greg Parks with our fourth shot, and Peter Forsberg beat me with a deke to the backhand, going five-hole between my legs to tie it up.

The shootout was 2–2 and we were going to our fifth and final round. Greg Johnson was stoned by Tommy Salo, and I had to stop Roger Hansson next or the game would be over.

I went with my strategy and got aggressive. As he came at me with speed, I matched him perfectly, skating backwards. I waited as he made the first move, and I followed him to my right. He had nowhere to go and shot it right into my pads.

Now it was sudden death.

The shooting order was switched up, so Sweden went first this time. The rules stated that a team could reuse any shooter from the first round in the sudden-death round.

First up was Svensson again. He had beaten me with speed the previous time, and I was determined not to let it happen again. Sure enough, he came at me with blazing speed. I got aggressive, but this time I was waiting for him. I backed off and matched his speed perfectly as he tried to deke me wide on almost the exact same move, and he missed the net.

Petr Nedved went again for us. All Petr had to do now was score and we would win gold. I went back to the bench thinking that Petr should shoot. He had an incredibly hard and deceptive wrist shot that, when he had time, was almost impossible to stop. I also knew the ice had had a full game and overtime played on it, so deking the goalie was a risky move.

Petr picked up the puck at centre ice and went down towards Tommy Salo. He deked Salo to his left, and he had Salo down and out. With the game-winner on the backhand of his stick, the puck flipped up at the last second on the bad ice, and it rolled off the end of Petr's stick wide of the net. I couldn't believe it. All Petr had to do was tap it in . . . and he missed.

Peter Forsberg was up next.

Forsberg picked up the puck at centre ice and came at me

with speed. As with all the others, I forced him to deke. I followed him as he took me to my right. I immediately thought, *I've got him. He's cut off with nowhere to go.*

But that's exactly when great players do *what great players do.* Peter shifted the puck wide over to his right, took his left hand off his stick and, with the extra length he got on his reach, reached around me on his backhand and tapped the puck towards the goal with only his right hand on his stick.

Oh shit!! my mind screamed out. I reached back to my left with my glove hand as far as I could, and I missed the puck by millimetres as it slid right under my glove. Peter Forsberg had scored on me one-handed. It was one of the greatest shootout goals of all time. (Words won't do it justice. That's what YouTube is for.)

We still had a chance to tie. Paul Kariya had scored earlier and had the chance to force an eighth shootout round. He skated in and Salo dove to his right. Paul went to fire a shot into the top right-hand corner, but it hit the top of Salo's pad and went wide.

Sweden were champions.

We got silver.

It was one of the greatest hockey games ever played in the Olympics.

Apparently, the Swedish coach asked Mats Näslund to take the seventh shot, but he refused. Håkan Loob also said no. Two veteran players with NHL experience, and Loob was a Stanley Cup champion. They were both too nervous to go. That's when Peter Forsberg stepped up and said, "I'll take it."

Peter Forsberg, a 20-year-old kid, went out on the ice in front of millions watching on television and made an incredible move to score on me to win the gold.

In hockey circles, the move is world-famous. It is known simply as *The Forsberg*.

Immediately after the Games were over, the Swedish government called my agent and asked him if they could make a national postage stamp of Forsberg scoring on me in the final. I wasn't sure how I felt about it. Forsberg agreed, of course, and they wanted to use my likeness too. Needless to say, I was in no mood. I said no thanks.

So they simply changed my likeness instead. The designer

was a guy named Lars Sjööblom, and he simply swapped the colour of my jersey from red to blue, took my name off the back, and changed the number from 1 to 11.

Some players get posterized. I got *postage stamped*.

(Thank you, Peter.)

Now, you might think that something like that would have sent me into a tailspin. But actually, I made peace with that game pretty quickly. That's one of the things that I am most proud of. I could have let *The Forsberg* define me. I could have let it destroy my NHL career before it ever really got started. I could have unravelled after Lillehammer. But I didn't. I got on the plane home from Norway frustrated but proud. Calm. Hopeful. Happy.

That loss didn't destroy me. Forsberg didn't destroy me.

Unfortunately, my true nemesis was always my own mind. And it was lying in wait.

I had no idea that just three months later, I would be standing around in that bar in DC with a Coors Light in my hand, and the *thought* would arrive. The wire would short-circuit. The dark loop would begin. And my life would never be the same.

6

I wish I could jump."

There's no walking those words back. Not when you say them to your own mother at the top of the Empire State Building, on what's supposed to be one of the greatest moments of your life. I wish I could unsay the words now, but I can't. It's a memory that I still carry around with me, and it's a stark reminder that whatever mental health statistics you see reported—no matter how large the number—don't do the problem justice. Mental illness is never just about that one person. The toll that it takes on families and friends is profound and can take years to heal, even after the person gets help.

Obviously, when I said those words, my mom was stunned. She started crying. And the most heartbreaking thing of all was that she had no idea what to do. Mental health was not something that was talked about in my mother's generation. It was swept under the rug and never discussed. If someone in a family was struggling with severe mental illness, they were often dropped off at the insane asylum, never to be seen again. And if they did come back, they came back a shell of the person they had been, due to the inhumane ways that we treated mental illness in the not-so-distant past. My mom grew up in the days of electroshock therapy and all those horror stories. At the Empire State Building, I remember her looking at me with so much confusion and helplessness. It breaks my heart to think about it now.

You may ask yourself why she didn't put me on the first plane back to Canada. But I was putting her in an impossible situation, because I was begging her not to tell anyone for fear of losing my career and living with the stigma for the rest of my life. It's easy to look at it now, with all we've learned, and think that she should have gotten me some help. But until you're in that situation, as a mother or a father, I don't think you can understand how hard it is.

She stayed with me as long as she could, but after a week in New York, she had to get back to her job in Calgary. She was so terrified to leave me alone after everything I had told her, but I promised her I wouldn't do anything stupid and that I would come back to Calgary as soon as the playoffs were over. I dropped her off at the airport, we hugged, she cried her eyes out, and off she went. I was alone again.

Alone, alone, alone. You can't imagine how alone. The hockey situation didn't help. Every day before practice, I would get dressed in my equipment, pray to God that no one would even look at me and see how bad I was struggling, then I'd go out on the ice and stand in the corner for the full hour of practice. Just in case somebody got hurt. No one ever did. I barely took a shot, ever. When practice was over, I'd get undressed and wait at my stall until long after the regulars were gone, and then go back to the hotel by myself. I became an expert at the bullshit excuse. Those were the days of pay phones, so I was the king of saying, "Sorry, I have to go make a call" any time a teammate came up to me to shoot the shit. All those lame excuses a person makes when they want to get out of somewhere quickly, I used them. *Whoops, forgot my stick over there. Whoops, have to go take a leak. Whoops, I better stretch out in the hall.* I barely got by. I was like a scared, sickly ghost, floating around the Garden. I was just counting the days to go home.

The only thing that saved my sanity during the playoffs was that I happened to become good friends with an MTV VJ known as Kennedy. If you're under 35, you probably just went "Who?" But if you're over 35, you probably just went, "KENNEDY!!!" She was a bit of a '90s icon. MTV had this show called *Alternative Nation*, which featured all the grunge music that was blowing up during that era, like Pearl Jam, Soundgarden and Nirvana, and Kennedy was the sarcastic, quirky host. We ended up becoming good friends and hung out during the playoffs, since she lived in Manhattan. I mean, I say we hung out, but half the time I wasn't even there. I was floating off in space somewhere. I remember one time grabbing dinner with Kennedy and her friend, and when the food came, I was spiralling out of control so badly that it was almost like everything went fuzzy. You know when old TVs used to go on the fritz? Well, the TV was me. I was just short-circuiting, and I couldn't eat, I couldn't even speak, I couldn't do anything but think my paranoid thoughts. *Dark, Dark, Dark, Dark, Dark, Dark, Oh God I better say something, they're looking at me, DarkDarkDarkDarkDarkDarkDarkDARKTheyknowtheyknowtheythinkyou're*

SICK

INSANE

BROKEN

TheyknowTheyknowTheyknowTheyknow.

I just remember the friend looking at me like I was crazy, and Kennedy being really cool about everything and making excuses for me. I don't think she ever knew it, but Kennedy was a rock for me. For the record, we never got together romantically, although the guys on the team had a field day with me about it. Kennedy was funny, kind and had a heart of gold. You never know how much you can mean to someone else just by *being there*. You could save a life and not even know it. If I hadn't had Kennedy during that time, who knows what would have happened. I probably would not be here right now. I was so, so sick. All I wanted to do was go home and, just my luck, the Stanley Cup Final against Vancouver went the full seven games. Between Games 6 and 7, there were three days to wait. It was the longest three days of my life. I booked my flight home for eight a.m. on June 15, the day after Game 7. Win or lose, I was on the first flight out of there the next day.

Finally, game day came. I had heard that a pair of tickets was going for $10,000 apiece. It was pandemonium in New York. I had two tickets and gave them to Kennedy so she could take a friend to the game. Because of the state I was in, most of the game was a blur. I remember it going right down to the wire. It's funny because I had spent so much of the playoffs sitting up in the box with the other black aces, just hoping we'd lose so I could get out of there. That's how desperate I was. It had nothing to do with the Rangers at all. I was just in pure despair. But by Game 7, I was finally going home either way, and I could finally find some semblance of joy in the moment. With three minutes to go in the game, I went down to ice level along with all the other emergency players. Being so close to the ice, and feeling the weight of the moment, I kind of broke out of the fog and realized how close I was to being able to hoist the Stanley Cup. In the dying seconds of the game, the Canucks had a faceoff in the Rangers end. We were up by a goal. They pulled their goalie for the extra attacker. It was the height of drama. Off the faceoff, the puck went into the Rangers corner, and all of a sudden the clock hit zero. The Rangers were finally Stanley Cup champions after 54 long years.

I was a Stanley Cup champion.

Somehow, I was actually a Stanley Cup champion.

Surreal would be an understatement, given the hell that I was living through. I rushed out onto the ice with the rest of the team before the Cup presentation. Despite my sickness, it was an experience of a lifetime. It was the one thing that felt truly magical. Not one fan left the building while the Cup was being passed around from player to player. It was pure elation across the city. Everything you dream of, but somehow it's real.

I invited Kennedy and her roommate to join me in the dressing room as the team celebrated. The locker room was packed with people, and I was just the emergency guy, so I stood at the back of the room and hopped on a bench where there were four or five cases of champagne. I kept grabbing bottles, one by one, popping corks, shaking and spraying them all over everyone's heads. Eventually, the Cup was passed over to me, and as I picked it up, I realized how heavy it is. The thing weighs 35 pounds! In your dreams, it's a hell of a lot lighter, that's for sure. I took a glorious sip of champagne out of the Stanley Cup. It was incredible. A bit tinny, but incredible.

I invited Kennedy to take her turn. She said that it tasted like grapefruit juice mixed with old feet, but that it was one of the sweetest moments of her life. I was so happy I got to share that experience with her, after everything she did for me, just by being a good friend.

As I left Madison Square Garden that night, it was really late, and outside on the streets there was an eerie calm over the city, almost like a massive wave of relief and euphoria. Some of the guys went out to party, but I drove back to the hotel and went to bed alone. For a brief moment, I had peace. I had lifted the Stanley Cup at the age of 21. My whole career was ahead of me. My whole life, too. I had money in the bank. I had friends and family who cared deeply about me. What was the problem? Why was I feeling so bad, anyway?

Hey, you know what? Maybe it was all going to be . . .

Nope.

As soon as my head hit the pillow and I closed my eyes, the dark thoughts returned. First a whisper. A reminder. *Hello, we're back.* Then louder and louder. Every time you ask them to go away, a little bit louder, faster, more cruel. Ceaseless. Endless. Screaming.

I was at the top of the world, and my brain was screaming at me:

Dark, dark, dark, dark, dark, fear, fear, fear, worry, dark, dark, dark, they'll know, they'll find out, why are you even thinking that? Why, why, why, darkness, darkness, walls are closing in, walls are closing in, dark, dark, dark . . .

I knew.

This is never going to go away, no matter what.

*

I was on the first flight home the next morning. It's amazing how fleeting the warm feelings are in your life whenever you're dealing with a mental health issue. Drinking out of the Stanley Cup was incredible, but I can't tell you how little it meant to me once I got home to Calgary. I was a mess and I desperately needed help. I had a lot of time on my hands in the off-season, without the routine of hockey to keep me distracted, and it had my brain in complete overdrive. One day, I don't know why exactly, but I just couldn't take it, anyway, and I finally grabbed the Yellow Pages. You remember the Yellow Pages, kids? Well, it was a thick book of business listings that existed before the internet came along. They literally had all the phone numbers listed in alphabetical order, like an encyclopedia (which was Wikipedia for old people).

I opened the Yellow Pages, flipped to *T* for "Therapists" and looked for the friendliest advertisement I could find. I had no clue what to look for. I thought therapists were like family doctors and that they all knew what they were doing and could help anyone. Boy, I couldn't have been more wrong. I found an ad that had some flowers and a nice message on it. *Looks friendly enough*, I thought. So I called and made an appointment.

And from that day on, my life completely turned around. Within one session, I was fixed. The therapist asked me a few questions, and suddenly it all made sense. I was okay. I was good.

That's the end of the book, folks. I hope you enjoyed it.

Yeah, no. Just kidding.

Unfortunately, this is not one of those kinds of mental health books. I don't have some simple three-step solution for you. I don't have a fairy-tale story. All I have is the raw truth. And the raw truth? Just reaching out for help that day did not instantly make all my problems go away. In fact, it was more like taking one small step on a journey of a million.

The Yellow Pages Therapist was not a good fit, to say the least. I went to her office for three or four weeks and had seven or eight sessions. She was, to be extremely nice about it, "old school" in her practices. We did hypnotherapy in one session, and in another, I took some strange written test that I didn't really understand, and I paid over $900 for it. It was literally one of those personality tests that you can take online now for free.

I was in complete despair, and she was telling me the equivalent of which Harry Potter house I belonged to. Over time, I started to open up to her a bit about some of my thoughts. It just all felt very odd. She kept bringing everything back to my sexuality, when the voices in my head were so much more complicated. Then came the worst thing that ever could have happened, given the way my brain worked.

The therapist actually contacted my mom. I don't think that's ethical or even legal, and it's certainly not appropriate, but for whatever reason she called my mom on the phone and told her that she found out what was wrong with me, and it was simple. "Usually people discover that they're gay much younger," she told my mom.

Even the way she said it was just so insensitive and petty. It crushed me. Not because I was homophobic. Not at all. God, I would have loved for that to have been the key to all my problems. But I knew in my heart that it *wasn't* it. I'd had a few girlfriends. I could appreciate that guys were handsome, but ultimately, I was attracted to women. Even back then, as sick as I was, I could sense that the intrusiveness of the sexual thoughts—especially the HIV thoughts—were not about the shame of the thing itself. It was not as simple as being ashamed that I was gay, or even confused by it. It was more about *other people* thinking I was gay, and the repercussions that would have on my career. What I didn't know at the time is that the nature of my illness actually has to do with the *opposite* of the thing that is in your heart. People who obsessively think about harming their newborn baby don't actually want to harm their newborn baby. People who can't stop thinking about swerving their car into the other lane don't actually want to do that. But the signals in their brain get crossed, and they hyper-focus on danger or loss or harm (in my case, the harm that being outed as gay would ruin my NHL career, or the harm that contracting HIV would kill my girlfriend, or the harm that picking up a knife at breakfast would cause me to snap).

I did not know that these thoughts had an underlying pattern. I did not know that my disease had a name. Unfortunately, neither did my Yellow Pages Therapist.

So when she told my mother that the answer was simply my sexuality, I was devastated and hopeless. It played into all my worst fears about reaching out for help. She not only gave me a diagnosis that I knew in my heart was not the answer, she betrayed my trust by calling my mother without telling me. Worst of all, she made me feel like the thoughts I was having had some *basis* to them. Like I had things in my life that I couldn't come to grips with, and that's what was fuelling the darkness. It was the worst thing that could have happened.

I mean, if what she's saying is that obsessive thoughts mean that something is true, then if I actually am gay and just not coming to terms with it, am I actually a psychopath because I can't stop thinking about the knives at breakfast? Do I want to hurt people? Am I totally insane? By her logic, all repetitive thoughts have meaning. The darkness is literal. It's all real. If you think about it, it's real.

My biggest fear all along, and the reason that I refused to tell anyone what was happening, was that these dark thoughts were all *true*. That I was choosing them. That they were the real me. Again, remember that this was 1994. Remember what the culture was like back then, and how we treated this stuff. Just think if you told your friend, "Hey man, you know what? I can't stop thinking about picking up that knife over there. I'm obsessing over it, because I don't want to hurt someone. The thought horrifies me. But I can't stop thinking about the knife."

Would they have said, "Oh man, it sounds like you're dealing with a mental health issue. We should find you some help"?

In 1994?

They would've said, "Dude, what the hell? Why are you telling me that? Are you a fucking psycho?"

I thought I was a psycho, let alone everybody else.

So when I finally worked up the courage and reached out to a professional and it all went badly, it sent me into a massive tailspin. I thought that if this professional therapist couldn't help me, nobody could. From that point on, suicide was always in the forefront of my mind. I was convinced that there was no hope, no help, and my life was doomed to be lived out inside the prison of my mind.

A few days later, I went to a friend's house. I was really fighting it, and my brain was firing hard on all cylinders. We were in the backyard, sitting on some lawn chairs and having a couple of beers, when he suggested we invite some people over to hang out. I agreed but told him I had to go back to my house real quick to change. I left his place, went back to my house, and without telling anyone, I impulsively packed up all my things. I got in my car and drove six hours to Kamloops. I never showed up to the party, never even told anyone I left town. I was in crisis, trying to run away from my thoughts.

When I got to Kamloops, I stayed with a former girlfriend. My brain was on fire, so I went back to what was familiar, and she made me feel safe. In the meantime, the darkness continued to bombard me every second of every day. I never had any peace. Of course, I still tried to hide what was going on in my head from my girlfriend.

Over the next few days, I spent countless hours at bookstores searching through the self-help section trying to self-diagnose and looking for stories that had any kind of hope in them—somebody who had been sick with mental illness but got better.

I found nothing.

I was completely discouraged and defeated. I swore to myself that one day, if I ever got better, I would make sure that people would hear my story and know that there is hope.

A few weeks went by in Kamloops, and I was at the end of my rope. The panic attacks and anxiety were becoming too much to bear. I had no set plan, but often thought of different ways to end my life. I mean, I had won a Stanley Cup and had no joy. I had reached out for help and had my trust betrayed. There was no name for whatever I was feeling. For whatever I was. I was truly, totally, utterly alone. I would never be "normal" again. At least that's what my brain kept screaming at me.

I went out for a few beers one night in early August with a friend and former teammate named Scott. I met him at a bar called Ned Kelly's. I was sitting there at a high-top table, not really talking or engaging in conversation, when a wave of emptiness came over me. The thoughts had disappeared, and not in a good way. I felt zero emotion. *Nothing*. I was emotionally dead inside. I excused myself and told Scott I had to leave. I got in my car and started driving aimlessly. I wasn't sure where I was going or what I was doing.

And that's how I ended up on that mountain road just after midnight, determined to drive my car off the cliff.

I just didn't want to exist anymore.

I shifted the car into first gear, released the clutch and hammered on the gas. I could hear the turbo kick in as it spun hard and loud. The torque sucked me into the back of my seat. The RPMs rose quickly. The engine was roaring. I pushed in the clutch and shifted into second gear, hammering the gas again. The car quickly hit 40 miles per hour.

I pushed the accelerator to the floor and shifted gears again. The needle on the speedometer leapt—60, 70, 80. There was no stopping me. I was locked in a zone as I stared straight ahead. 120, 130, 140. I was hurtling towards the end of the road. In the distance, I could see a yellow sign signalling the turn in the road.

And then . . . something stopped me.

A *what if?* thought.

And no, it really was not profound. It was not a message from God. It was not even particularly interesting.

It was simply, *What if you go over the edge and you* don't *die? What if they find you mangled but still alive? What if you're trapped inside your brain,* and *inside your body?*

Two prisons instead of one.

Literally, that thought horrified me so much that I slammed on the brakes as hard as I could. I was 200 feet from the edge when the car finally stopped. Just 200 feet from oblivion. Just five seconds away from being a statistic. There is obviously a dark irony here. All these horrifying, sinister *what if?* thoughts were torturing me daily, ruining my life . . . and yet one floated down from the heavens out of nowhere and saved my life.

I just sat there in shock. My hands were shaking on the steering wheel as I started to realize the magnitude of what had just happened. I started sobbing uncontrollably, yelling out loud for someone to help me.

After a long time, I finally gathered myself, turned the car around and headed home. I pulled into the driveway at my girlfriend's house, got out and went inside. She had been in bed sleeping and was facing away from me as I crawled into bed beside her. Still in my clothes, I cuddled up to her back and put my arm around her. She had no idea what had taken place just a few minutes before. Mentally drained and exhausted, I fell asleep.

The next morning, I woke up to a new day. The world was

still there. The sun was up. And that's when I made the decision that I would just live with whatever it was in my head and hope to figure it out one day.

I never told anybody about that night, ever. No one.

I wasn't ready to die. I just didn't know how to go on living. So I went into purgatory.

7

There's a 900-pound elephant in the room, isn't there?

I can see that now, reliving all of this. It seems implausible, right? I mean, at this point in the story, how in the world does someone who is suicidal, manic, practically starving himself to death, suffering from insomnia, and barely functioning well enough to get out of bed and pull on his pants in the morning play another game in the National Hockey League—let alone play for a few more *years*?

It's a great question. I'm not even sure I have the answer. A lot of this period of my life is a blur. After my suicide attempt in Kamloops, the next month went by with no resolution to my torturous thoughts. I spent hours upon hours ruminating daily trying to figure them out, like they were some kind of complex math equation. You know that famous Twitter meme with the guy from *It's Always Sunny in Philadelphia* with all the string zigzagging everywhere connecting all the little index cards, like he's trying to solve a conspiracy? That was me, except I didn't even write anything down. I was maniacally trying to solve the conspiracy inside my own head, all day, every day.

The odd time I would get a temporary answer that would hold my anxiety at bay, it would usually last for about two minutes, tops. Then the thoughts would rebound in another direction and there would be a new self-torturing puzzle to figure out. I survived by avoiding triggers as best I could and keeping myself as busy as possible. If I wasn't in bed, I would always be moving. Either pacing around the room or going for walks or driving in my car. Anything that would semi-occupy my mind. I was learning to survive in my own brain, by any means necessary. Of course, being on the ice was always the best. Nothing focuses the mind quite like a puck fizzing by your head at 90 miles an hour.

Unfortunately for me, after that summer from hell, when I was at my lowest moment, the NHL went on hiatus. There was a labour dispute, and the owners insisted on capping the increasing salaries of players and assisting franchises in weaker markets. The players wanted collective bargaining. I don't know who was right, but in the end, money trumped the good of the game. The NHL was locked out. That meant only one thing for a young player like me: Not the beach. The minors.

Back to beautiful Binghamton.

My girlfriend and I made the decision that she would come live with me for the season. She had recently graduated from nursing school, and it was difficult for nurses to land jobs in Canada, but there was a shortage of nurses in the States. We were able to get her a work visa to come to the US with me and get nursing experience. It was a win-win for both of us. We moved into a townhouse where no one lived above me. It was quiet. My anxiety about the footsteps was gone. I wasn't alone, which helped me from spiralling completely. At least I had someone there who I had to hide everything from. That alone was almost a distraction in itself. With her by my side and a stable living environment, I was able to temporarily function and survive.

It was also calming to be off the Rangers' radar. Or so I thought. It was probably naive of me to think that the Rangers weren't aware that something was seriously wrong. That lockout season, I was playing well in the minors, but the team would have received regular reports on my odd behaviour. I was late for meetings, late for practices, not eating properly, not sleeping properly, not working out with the team. I'm sure it looked terrible. I used all my energy just to be able to get out onto the ice. Once I was on the ice, the switch was flipped, and I went into Goalie Mode autopilot. My teammates liked me well enough, but obviously some thought I was selfish and arrogant. I never went to team dinners. I didn't ask anyone anything about themselves. If I was taping my stick in the dressing room and someone tried to come up to shoot the shit, I would be lost so deep in my mind trying to solve the conspiracy that I'd barely even hear what they said. The sound would come at me all muffled, and I'd just look at them in a daze and shrug my shoulders or walk away like I had forgotten something.

My mind robbed me of everything good in life. It stole my ability to maintain relationships and friendships, or feeling any form of joy, however small. It made me look bad in the eyes of others when all I was trying to do was survive and stay alive each day. I don't know how it didn't rob me of my career. Somehow, I wasn't blackballed. I was definitely considered damaged goods, but I was talented enough to stay afloat. I never breathed a word of my sickness to the Rangers—but, I mean, who in their right mind blows off a Stanley Cup tickertape parade in Manhattan? I was still considered a top prospect, but they knew I had no chance to play in New York. A trade would be the only way out. Send the kid to some GM who doesn't know how screwed up he is yet! Another goalie "head case"! I don't fault the Rangers, but knowing what the culture was like, I can just hear the way they probably talked about me back then.

The NHL lockout lasted from October 1994 until January 1995 and when it was over they could only play a shortened 48-game season. It was disastrous for fans and for a lot of players. At least in Binghamton, I was getting paid and playing. We finished first in our division and third overall. I literally do not remember most of it, but somehow, I had another good season in the minors.

I hadn't heard from the Rangers much through that season, but as the trade deadline approached, talks had started to pick up. Neil Smith, the GM in New York, referred to me as a "blue-chip prospect," but added that my trade value wasn't as high as that of Alexei Kovalev, Mattias Norström or Sergei Zubov, who other NHL teams were calling about. Nevertheless, the rumours floated around. I waited nervously all day and at the last minute before the trade deadline expired at three p.m. Eastern, the phone rang. It was the assistant general manager, Larry Pleau. He told me I had been traded to Vancouver, thanked me for my time and wished me the best of luck. That was it. I was going back home to Canada. I was going to a new city. I was going to a dressing room where the guys didn't see me as the lonely weirdo who doesn't talk to anybody. I was getting a fresh start.

Hey, what could go wrong?

After the trade, the Canucks didn't have any room for me on their teams anywhere. Kay Whitmore was the backup to Kirk McLean in Vancouver, and Mike Fountain was the number one with Syracuse, their minor league affiliate. There were still a few weeks left in the season, and they were unsure where to put me. I was in limbo. That's when Tom Renney and Hockey Canada came calling again for me to lead Canada at the World Championships in Sweden. I got on a plane and met the team in Prague. It's one of my favourite cities in the world. My girlfriend stayed behind in Binghamton to work. I was still sick and trying to figure out the puzzle to my thoughts, but I was functioning. The severity of the anxiety would come and go in waves. I had learned how to survive during those times by avoiding triggering things and finding ways to make excuses.

We played a few exhibition games and then flew to Sweden for the tournament. That's when I was visited by a completely new demon. (Just when you think you're safe, there's always a twist.) Credential day was pure hell. My repetitive thoughts flared up as names of different players kept popping up in my head. Names, names, names. New names. Interesting names. Different names. Names, names, names. Repeating over and over again in my head. I couldn't understand what was happening, and I started to question what it meant. The tsunami of anxiety was crushing me, and the repeating of names in my head shifted from person to person.

FIRST NAME LAST NAME

FIRST NAME LAST NAME

FIRSTNAMEFIRSTNAMEFIRSTNAME

LASTNAMELASTNAMELASTNAMELASTNAME-LASTNAME

"Corey, you okay, man?"

FIRSTNAMEFIRSTNAMEFIRSTNAME

LASTNAMELASTNAMELASTNAMELASTNAME-LASTNAME

DIFFERENT NAME DIFFERENT NAME

BACK TO THE OTHER NAME, OTHER NAME, OTHER NAME, OTHER NAME

FIRSTNAMEFIRSTNAMEFIRSTNAME

LASTNAMELASTNAMELASTNAMELASTNAME-LASTNAME

FIRSTNAMEFIRSTNAMEFIRSTNAME

LASTNAMELASTNAMELASTNAMELASTNAME-
LASTNAME

Stopstopstopstopstop FocusPullyourselftogether

FIRSTNAMEFIRSTNAMEFIRSTNAME

LASTNAMELASTNAMELASTNAMELASTNAME-
LASTNAME

It was a confusing new twist with the same repetitive *what if?* puzzle. I couldn't make it stop. I was unsure how I would keep it together, but once the tournament started, focusing on hockey kept my mind busy. We didn't have a very good team, but I was playing well, and we somehow came together as a team through the round-robin to beat the United States in the quarter-final. It led us to another showdown with Sweden in the semifinal, just one year after our loss to them at the Olympics. Personally, I had a chance at some form of redemption. Deadlocked at two at the end of regulation time, Daniel Alfredsson, who would go on to be a legendary Ottawa Senators player, scored over my glove side and won the game in overtime.

(Thanks again, Sweden. It wasn't enough for me to be a stamp, eh?)

We had to settle for playing against the Czechs for the bronze. It was disappointing, but I was excited to have a chance at a medal from the World Championships to take home. We beat the Czechs 4–1 in the bronze medal game, and I took home my second medal while suffering from severe untreated mental illness. How's that for "weak"?

After the success at the World Championships, I was excited for a fresh start with the Canucks. I was told to come to training camp but that I would have to earn a spot. I spent the summer of 1995 training hard and was ready. I went to Vancouver a month prior to camp, paid my own way and got myself in the best shape I could. I was determined to play in the NHL. The thoughts weren't gone. They were always there, lurking. They returned the second I sat still. A name or a word would always repeat incessantly in the back of my mind, almost as if it was on autopilot. I could never stop it. It was just *there*. There, there, there, there, name, name, name, name, name. It's so there that you don't even have time to tell yourself not to think about it. It's already happened. Now it's already happened again. It's gone already, and it's already back. It's *there*.

At least when I was on the ice, I could shift the obsessive thoughts towards the puck. I played very well during training camp, and I felt like I had a good chance to stick around. I felt like I had proved that I was an NHL goalie (and a functioning human in the locker room). Then it happened . . . well, almost. Right at the end of training camp, I was stretching on the ice in the corner with a couple of other rookies, Scott Walker and Dean Malkoc. Rick Ley, the Canucks head coach, skated over towards us, and I got nervous. *Here it comes,* I thought. *The moment of truth. Either I'm getting sent down again or getting a place to live.* Rick Ley looked at me for a second, then veered away and went over to Scott and Dean. He told them they had the go-ahead to find a place to live. They had made the team. He didn't look back at me and skated away. I started nervously laughing inside. I wasn't sure what that meant. Did they make it and I didn't?

The next morning, before the final practice, Kay Whitmore was put on waivers for possible reassignment to the minors, and Ley came up to me again.

"All right, go find a place to live."

It was bittersweet to beat out another goalie for the job, especially when it was a guy as good as Whit, but there can only be two goalies on a team, and that's just the business.

I was officially a Canuck.

I found an apartment in downtown Vancouver in a high-rise building made of solid cement. When I secured my lease and got the keys, I found myself lying on the empty bedroom floor in tears. I was so terrified of what had happened in Binghamton with the footsteps happening again, so I lay there listening intently to see if I could hear anything that would set me off. After three hours of lying on the floor of my empty apartment, I happily deemed it to be silent enough to live in.

The best part of being in a new situation in Vancouver was that I didn't have much time to sit and think. I was coping really well at first, but I remember my parents coming to visit me, and my mom would try to talk to me and I'd just be *somewhere else*. She'd say to my dad, "Oh, Corey's in that other world now."

That became the norm for me. I'd be with my friends somewhere doing something and I'd simply disappear inside myself. Or I'd literally disappear completely and leave without telling anyone. I was the king of the phantom exit. It was like a magic trick—one second everything is normal and you think we're having a good time. Then *poof*, I'm gone. It was difficult to focus on anything, and I continually had that feeling of needing to get out of whatever situation I was in—almost like I was an animal that was about to be cornered. It was extremely hard to stay engaged in a conversation. I didn't like looking people in the eye, because I felt trapped. I'm sure at times people thought I was an asshole or didn't care, when it was actually just the opposite. I cared so much about people and what they thought of me, and I was being bombarded with anxiety and relentless intrusive thoughts left and right.

That season, I came in as the backup. Kirk McLean had been the Canucks starter for seven years. He was a key reason that Vancouver went on the run to the Stanley Cup Final in '94. Kirk was a good guy, but we didn't hang out or have much of a relationship. I knew my role, but my goal was to be the number one. I continually pushed Kirk to take over his job. That's just the business. Goaltending is always a tough balance. It made it difficult to cheer for the other guy to play well, because if he did,

I didn't get to play (and in my case, get the added bonus of 60 minutes of peace from my brain). It's hard to set your ego aside when you want the net.

Whenever I got in the net that season, I was determined to make my mark. And when most fans think of the name Corey Hirsch, they probably think of that season. But maybe not for what I did between the pipes. They probably think of my iconic goalie mask.

Okay, let's talk about the *Psycho* mask.

Half the people reading this don't know what the heck I'm talking about, and the other half just got really excited. As a bit of a goalie mask connoisseur myself, I have to say that I think it was probably one of the most badass designs ever made. It's the meaning behind the design that makes it what it is. The darkness of that mask was *real*. I just wish that I wasn't the one who lived it.

Being on a new team, I needed a new goalie mask. This is, absolutely and without a doubt, the best part of being a goalie. Yes, you have to step in front of 100-mile-an-hour slapshots. But on the bright side, every single season you get a fresh white mask that you can paint extremely cool shit on. What could be better?

I knew that it was going to be hard to top my Rangers mask. It had King Kong climbing up the side of the Empire State building, and the detail was amazing. It was done by a friend of mine who was an Itech painter, Frank Cipra. I got traded to Vancouver a short time after I got it, and only wore it a handful of times. So I really wanted my Vancouver mask designed with something special. And the problem was local inspiration. I couldn't figure out what the hell was on the front of that Canucks jersey. It looked like a mangled trumpet to me, and I honestly didn't comprehend that it was supposed to be a skate! So then I started thinking about the team colours—black, red and yellow—and I realized that they were synonymous with Halloween. That's how it all started. As a kid, I'd loved the scary masks, especially the one worn by Gary Bromley. When Gary played with the Canucks at the start of the 1980s, his nickname was "Bones" and his mask was painted so that it looked like a human skull.

I called up Frank and said that I wanted a design that was dark and scary. When I told him about my idea, the Alfred

Hitchcock movie *Psycho* popped into his head. Frank asked me if I liked horror movies, and I said of course. I left the rest to Frank to design, and when I unboxed it for the first time, I got goosebumps.

If you know it, you *know* it:

The brick walkway leading up to the haunted Bates Motel with Norman's mother creeping in the window, backlit in yellow. The way he painted the motel on both sides of the mask was all warped and mirrored. It was like a funhouse mirror of hell. Then he had Alfred Hitchcock in a scary silhouette right in the middle. The dark sky looked like it was engulfed in fire. It looked *demonic*. It was perfect. It was *me*.

When I suffered from anxiety, it always felt as though my brain was on fire and about to explode. Frank had no idea what I was going through mentally, but the paint job captured it better than any words can describe. If you really want to know what it felt like to be inside my brain, just look at a picture of that mask.

I thought I was the only person in the world who felt that way. I couldn't have been more wrong. That season, I became good friends with "Almo," the great Alexander Mogilny, and we hung out a lot. I think we connected well with each other because of having similar anxiety issues. While in Buffalo, it was well known that Alex had a horrible fear of flying. He wouldn't fly with the team and at times would take a limo to and from road games. Although I never told him what I was going through, we understood each other. Alex was a kind, non-judgmental soul with a quiet personality who didn't let many people in. He was also the best player I ever played with in the NHL.

I didn't play much in the first half of the season, but in January, Kirk tore the cartilage in his left knee and would be out four to six weeks. I saw it as my chance to get my foot in the door for the starting job. With Kirk's injury, I was thrown into the fire, and I was determined to take over. Every time I put on the *Psycho* mask, I became someone else. I was locked in and I played extremely well that season. My issues were not gone, but I was always distracted, flying from game to game, and I didn't have too much idle time for my brain to go into overdrive.

We limped into the playoffs, but at least I got my first taste of real playoff hockey. We ended up losing to the eventual Stanley Cup champions, the Colorado Avalanche, in the first round. There was no denying Sakic, Forsberg and Roy that season. I was at peace with it, just like with the Olympics. And despite the hell that I was in, I was proud of myself. Somehow, some way, I had gone 17–14–6 in net during the season. I was an absolute mess off the ice, but on the ice, despite having a serious mental health issue, I won more games than I'd lost.

Not only had I made the Vancouver Canucks that year, I was named to the NHL All-Rookie Team. With what I was dealing with and going through, it was incredible what I had accomplished. I was able to set aside panic attacks, anxiety, sleeplessness, depression and disturbing repetitive thoughts, and still do my job at the highest level possible.

So don't ever tell me that having mental health problems makes a person weak. I was fighting a war every single day. I was surviving. I refused to break down. I just kept going. I was going to do it all on my own. And that was part of the problem.

8

The Cranberries changed everything.

Remember them? "Zombie"?

I wasn't even a big fan, to be honest. But 1996 was the summer of the Cranberries. They were everywhere. And it just so happened that a few weeks after the season ended, I broke up with my girlfriend. Although I loved her and I really appreciated how much she had been there for me during my lowest moments, I knew in my heart that I was not "in love" with her. I was simply too much of a mess to be what she needed me to be. She needed to live her life and find someone who could love her the way she deserved. So we parted ways.

All that summer, I hung out with my teammate Dean Malkoc quite a bit since we were both single. He lived in the apartment across from me and we would go out from time to time, but no matter how hard I tried, I couldn't find a girl who I could fall in love with. I would be attracted to a girl, and then my brain would completely ruin it for me the best way it knew how—through sabotaging my thoughts with repetitive negative *what if?* questions of hurting someone or having HIV or whatever new evil it invented for me that day.

It was almost like every time I started getting close to someone, my brain would say, *Oh no. No, no, no. You're staying right here with me, buddy. You don't need anybody else. You'll only let them down. You'll only end up hurting them. It's just you and me, man. We have to stay in the darkness* together.

I was ready to give up all hope when a friend of mine who booked the concerts at GM Place in Vancouver offered me two tickets to the Cranberries concert. I didn't know if I wanted to go. But he said, "Come on. My girlfriend is coming with me and she's bringing a friend. Why don't you come?" I had nothing to do that night, so I thought, *Hey, what the hell*. I showed up at the concert and met "the friend."

She was beautiful. There was just something different about her. It immediately lit a spark in me. We hung out all night, and I could feel that it was something real. We started dating right away, but I was still struggling with the doubts and irrational fears. In a sinister way, having someone I deeply cared about almost became a trigger in itself. If you have love, now you *really* have something to lose, right? When you were alone, it was just you dangling over the void. Now you feel like you're dangling with someone else, attached at the hip, and it's all your fault. You made the choice to bring them into this. You're responsible. You're going to ruin their life now, too. It's all your fault. Your fault your fault your fault your fault.

(And on and on.)

The tsunami waves of anxiety and panic were back. Confusion. Darkness. Puzzles. I spent countless hours trying to figure it out. I was euphoric and in the lust stage of the relationship, but my worlds were starting to collide now. I knew underneath it all that I wasn't gay, and I didn't have HIV, and I didn't want to hurt anyone. I *knew* it, in the deepest core of my soul. But when you have a mental illness, it's not about what you feel in your soul. It's not about the rational. You can try to tell yourself to be rational all day, and your brain will only laugh at you. Oh, you're a millionaire? You're going to lose it all. You have 100 friends? They all secretly resent you. Things are going well in your job? They're going to fire you any day now. The sky looks blue? It's green.

It's nearly impossible to explain to someone who hasn't experienced it first-hand. Because not only is the sky green, it's greener than green. It's always been green. Anyone who sees it as blue is lying to you. They're secretly laughing at you. It's obviously green. Green, green, green, green. Green until the word *green* doesn't even mean anything anymore, and it is just a sound, a tone, a scream, repeating over and over at 100 volume, forever.

All day long, you think about how green the sky is. You look at it 7,000 times. You stew and you obsess over it. It's green.

All the while, you're trying to pretend to your new girlfriend that everything is okay. You're normal! You're in love! It's all good! Oh, sorry, you were just lost in thought. That's all! Sorry! What were you saying again?

The cruel thing about mental illness is that you get so used to the suffering that it's almost easier to be alone. When you hurt someone else with your suffering, it's 10 times as brutal. So you look for every excuse in the world to self-sabotage every relationship and friendship that you have.

That season, everything went off the rails. After a year of relative peace, the massive storm in my brain was finally catching up to me again. The irony is that the harder I fought, and the more that I tried to "be normal" and "think like a normal person," the stronger the anxiety and the thoughts would get. I couldn't figure it out. I was in a nosedive, and it felt like there was no way out. Hockey brought me no joy or sense of accomplishment. Only fear. I wanted to quit.

Things went south really quickly that season. I was barely making it in time for practice. Every second that I could be alone with my dark thoughts was like gold to me. I had it timed so that if I left my apartment exactly four minutes prior to having to be at the rink, I could make it just in time for meetings. It was like every second was precious. Every millisecond that I didn't have to be around people was *safety*.

I was continually late for practices, for team meetings, film sessions, everything. I had withdrawn from my teammates. Some guys tried to reach out to me, but I wasn't saying a word. They all knew that I was suffering with something—drugs, women, whatever. Most of them thought it was based on my new relationship, and I don't blame them, because I stuck next to my girlfriend as much as I possibly could.

I was barely functioning. I couldn't eat, I didn't sleep, and I lost a ton of weight. I dropped 25 pounds in a few months and was down to 140 pounds trying to play goalie in the NHL. My equipment was hanging off me. I had bags under my eyes. I was pale as hell. I was genuinely wasting away before everyone's eyes. It was truly scary.

By then, it was becoming impossible to hide my mental illness. It was no longer just hidden in my brain. You could *see* it. One day after practice, I stepped out of the shower with a towel around my waist when Marty Gelinas was passing by. He looked at me and saw that I was skin and bones. He said,

"Hirschey, what's wrong with you?" I just put my head down and scurried by. I was like Gollum from *Lord of the Rings*. Just scurrying around the rink, trying to hide from everyone and talking to myself in my head.

Obviously, people asked questions. But I was lying through my teeth, trying to contain the damage everywhere. I was crazy in love with my girlfriend, and yet one side of my brain was telling me, *What if you don't really love this woman? What if you have AIDS and give it to her? What if you hurt her? Dark, dark, dark, dark.* And on and on and on and on. If it's repetitive to read it, imagine living it.

It was a relentless barrage of lies in my brain, and I was spiralling quickly into total paranoia. The danger felt so *real*. The harm was just around that next corner. It got worse, then a lot worse. Then one night everything went totally off the rails. For me, it's all a blur. But it's been pieced together over the years by friends.

Adrian Aucoin and his girlfriend used to hang out with me and my girlfriend, especially that first season in Vancouver. But as I was spiralling, we weren't hanging out as much. On one of the first road trips of the season, the whole team went out for beers. I wasn't there. I stayed in my room, spiralling. When Adrian got back to his hotel room around two a.m., his roommate told him he had to call his girlfriend immediately. It was pre-cellphone, and she had tried calling Adrian several times through the night. When Adrian called her back, she told him that I had been calling her in a panic, begging her to go check on my girlfriend back home in Vancouver.

I don't really remember any of this. I was in a dissociative state at the time. But apparently, I had tried calling my girlfriend, and she didn't pick up the phone. Of course, a normal brain would think, *Oh well, I guess she fell asleep.*

But my brain went straight to every catastrophic scenario it could conjure up.

There was a fire. She's dead. She's dead. She tried to change a light bulb and she fell off the chair and broke her neck. She's lying there on the floor, all alone. There was a carbon monoxide leak. She was murdered. She's dead. She's dead. My God, she's dead.

When I'm in that manic state, I have so many horrific, vivid, repetitive thoughts firing at 10 million miles an hour. And to me, the thoughts seem so *real*. Graphic images of her dead on the floor, repeating over and over. Blood. Horror movie images. It's so real that I don't even think of it as part of my imagination. It's already happened. So I called Adrian's girlfriend in a panic, begging her to go to my apartment, knock, buzz, go through the garage—whatever—to find my girlfriend.

I was in such a frantic state, and believed so deeply that she was really dead, that I ended up calling the police as well. Who knows who else I called, or what I did. I was in another world. When Adrian's girlfriend finally got a hold of my girlfriend, it turned out that she had fallen asleep with the ringer off. It was a nothing situation. It was so incredibly embarrassing. I was completely unravelling.

That was the first time Adrian or any of my teammates fully realized the extent of what I was dealing with. The cat was out of the bag, but nobody knew how to help me. The anxiety and shame were drowning me. I didn't think I could continue living. I couldn't get out of bed. I was non-functional. I was at the final crossroads. I told myself that I had one of two choices. I could finally tell someone what was going on *for real, 100 percent, no bullshit, everything, everything, everything* . . . or I was going to end my life.

A couple of days later, we were playing the New York Islanders in Nassau County, and being back in New York was a major trigger for me since that's where it all started. I got to the rink early and I pulled Canucks trainer Mike Burnstein aside and asked if we could talk privately. I had debated whether I should talk to him all night long and hadn't slept a wink. But at that point, I simply couldn't run from my brain any longer.

We walked outside the locker room to a spot under the stands in the bowels of the Nassau Coliseum. I found a private spot as far from the dressing room as I could find. I didn't want anyone to hear. I looked at Mike and I broke down. I was so deeply embarrassed, ashamed, exhausted and just plain broken. Through my tears, I told him the words that I wish I would have said years before:

"Mike, I need help. I really need some *help*, buddy. It's really bad. It's so bad that I'm thinking about ending my life."

Mike looked as though he was in shock. I don't think he had

ever been approached by any player and hit with anything like that. He said that he would talk to someone and find out how to get me some help. I begged him not to tell anyone on the team. Not even the coaches. Just like with my mom, I'd put him in an impossible situation, and he agreed.

Believe it or not, I got the start that night, and I actually went out and played. Of course, I couldn't stop anything. I let in five goals and even got into a fight. We lost 5–4 in overtime. The good news was that prior to the game, Mike contacted the team psychiatrist back in Vancouver to get the wheels in motion to get me some help. We bused to New Jersey after the game. I went to my hotel room, put my head on the pillow and cried myself to sleep, pleading with God to help me.

That's when I truly and completely broke.

We played New Jersey the next night, and when I went out for the morning skate, it was like my brain and my body had completely given out, after fighting so hard for so long. When I took the first drill, I couldn't see the pucks. They were whizzing by me. My vision was completely blurred. It was indescribable. It was almost like an out-of-body experience. It felt like I could watch myself playing goalie from above. Like my brain was somewhere five feet above my body, floating.

I was just standing there like a statue, frozen. Pucks were flying by me, or hitting me in the chest, and I wasn't even reacting. My body was in one place, and my mind was physically somewhere else. I didn't know what was happening. I thought I was dreaming or dead. I later found out that I was experiencing a syndrome called depersonalization. It was as though my brain was dealing with such a surge of anxiety that it had an electrical overload and needed to shut down. I went over to my coach, Tom Renney. I pulled him aside and said, "Tom, I can't do this anymore. I can't play."

Tom had witnessed me not reacting to pucks very early on at the rink at our morning skate, and it was clear to him I wasn't doing well. After I spoke to Tom, he said he'd cover for me with the team and that they would get me some help. The problem was, I was supposed to start that night. So Tom called an emergency team meeting in the dressing room after the morning skate. I sat in a corner with my head in my hands. I didn't want to look at anyone. He told the team that Mike Fountain, who was backing me up, was going to start that night in goal. It would be his first NHL game.

Tom told the boys, "If anyone in the media or around the team asks what's going on, we're going to tell them Hirschey's sick."

They knew that something was seriously wrong. I was so embarrassed and ashamed. I could sense all my teammates looking at me, and I could barely lift my head up. I was a 140-pound skeleton. I was almost in the fetal position in the corner of the dressing room.

I showered, changed, got on the team bus and sat in an empty seat up front, away from everyone. I sat there with my head in my hands, knowing full well that as my teammates awkwardly shuffled by one by one, not saying anything to me, I had just thrown away my NHL career. I had never in my life felt more alone.

That afternoon, the team psychiatrist in Vancouver called my hotel room, and I was so broken that I didn't even bother trying to hold anything back to check myself. I immediately spilled my guts to her about every detail. I didn't care anymore. I had to know what was happening or I was going to kill myself. I'm not sure how the rest of that trip would have played out if I hadn't received that call from her. Just her calling me and me saying the words out loud to her and unburdening myself ended up reducing my anxiety by half. She told me that when I got back to Vancouver, she was going to get me some real help.

We flew back to Vancouver, and I met a new psychologist a few days later. I was terrified of what I would find out, but I needed to know the truth. Was I a psychopath? Was I going to harm someone? All those *what if?* questions that had haunted me for so many years. My brain used to tell me that if I got help and told anyone the thoughts that were going through my mind, I would be thrown in jail forever. In a sense, my own brain was my abuser.

There was a knock at my door. I opened it and put on my most convincing fake smile as I welcomed the psychologist to my home. He came to my apartment because it was private and I thought there was a stigma to being seen going to a therapist's office. He took off his coat, walked in and sat down on my couch. He said, "Tell me what's happening."

All my walls came down. I told him everything. All my embarrassing, horrendous, bizarre thoughts. The violent thoughts, the sexually intrusive thoughts, the religious ones, and finally the self-harm thoughts as well.

After about 40 minutes, he stopped me, put down his paper and pen and took off his glasses and said the words that changed my life: "Corey, you're not a monster. And you aren't going to hurt anyone. I believe you have what's known as Obsessive-Compulsive Disorder. OCD."

OCD.

With those three simple letters, it felt like a 747 airliner had rolled off my chest. I started bawling in front of him. Within 40 minutes, I was diagnosed. I had been hiding my secret from friends and family, went through the embarrassment of being exposed in the dressing room, lost all that weight, withdrew from my teammates, lost many friends, and all I had to do was reach out, talk to somebody.

He went on to say that OCD isn't curable, but with the right therapy and the right medication, it's very treatable. I was just so happy to have an *answer*. It eased my mind so much knowing that there was a name for what I had been going through, and that there was a reason for my thoughts, and that I wasn't a monster.

But you know what's so cruel about OCD? The euphoria lasted for about a day. And then the demon started whispering to me . . .

That therapist?

He's lying.

He's trying to trick you.

He's lying to you. They're all lying to you.

The whisper got louder and louder and louder.

He's lying to you. Everyone is lying to you. You are sick. You are twisted. Dark, dark, dark, dark, dark, dark, dark, dark, the walls are closing in, they're lying to you, dark, dark, dark, dark, dark, liars, liars, liars, liars, the walls are closing, closing, closing, it's all true it's all true it's all true it's all true, IT'S ALL TRUE.

9

Okay, let's pause here for a minute.

I know most people think of OCD as "the hand washing thing" or "the light switch thing." They've probably seen
representations of it on TV. It's always the neurotic friend who
is worried about how their books are lined up on the shelf, or
how the pencil has to be at a perfect angle on the desk. Maybe
they have to flick the light switch on and off three times every
time they come into the room. And it's true that all that stuff can
be a part of OCD, for sure. But that's all just the surface-level

manifestations of a big, dark hole that can go deeper than you could ever imagine.

It's worth really thinking about that one word—*obsessive*.

People use it all the time now on social media, in a positive way. *Oh, I'm obsessed with that movie. I'm obsessed with fantasy football. I'm obsessed with that band.* A lot of athletes even use it to describe how hard they train, and entrepreneurs throw it around in interviews to brag about how much of their time they give to building their start-ups.

Obsessive.

It's equated with greatness. Our culture has almost turned this word into a skill that you put on your LinkedIn page or your college application. But Obsessive-Compulsive Disorder is a whole different animal. Believe me when I tell you that you do not want to experience *obsession* the way someone with OCD does. There is no off button. There is no volume control. There is no vacation. It is not a choice.

Having OCD was not a superpower. It didn't help me be a better goalie. It didn't help me succeed in life. It was just pure hell. It ruined almost every relationship I've ever had. It convinced me that I was a psychopath capable of hurting everyone I ever loved. It twisted every single pure thought that I had into something sinister and paranoid and shameful. The dark irony of OCD is that because of the nature of the beast, once you are diagnosed and you get professional help, your brain simply goes into overdrive trying to convince you that everything the professionals are telling you is a complete and utter lie. In fact, you don't really have OCD at all. The diagnosis was just another trick. You're actually just insane. You're damaged. The doctors are all frauds who don't understand what's really going on in your brain. I mean, how *could* they? They're not you. They're not experiencing this. They're full of shit. No one has ever understood you your entire life, and it's not going to start now. You're alone. You'll always be alone. These thoughts will never end. You will never know peace. You are trapped in this prison forever. And, you know what? As a matter of fact? You *deserve* all this. It's your fault. Dark people think dark thoughts. This is a choice. You are a monster. (Do you see how this works?)

If it was depressing and exhausting to read that paragraph, just imagine *living* it, on repeat, all day, every day, for years and years.

Once I got my OCD diagnosis, it was not a happy ending. The credits didn't roll. It was just another step up the mountain. It was the beginning of years of therapy and relief and triggers and setbacks and ups and downs. That's the reality of mental health that not a lot of people want to tell you about. Reaching out is the most important thing you can ever do. It can save your life. But it's not the end. It's the start of a journey, and that's okay. It's more than okay.

For my entire career, the only people I told about my diagnosis were my parents and my girlfriend. I hid my OCD from my coaches and teammates and everyone else in the hockey world. At the time, in the mid-'90s, it just felt like it would've been a death sentence for my career. I mean, the words "mental health" in an NHL locker room in 1996? Forget it.

"Mental health? Mental *what*? Jesus Christ, put this guy in the psych ward. Get his crazy ass out of here. This is a hockey team."

I was terrified of the stigma, so I tried to hide it like nothing had happened and nothing was wrong. Sometimes I wonder what would have happened if I had just told everyone the truth. Because that was the start of an extremely lonely

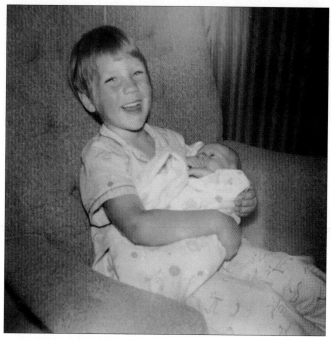

Me as a baby, with my older brother, Stacey.

I watched *Hockey Night in Canada* with my dad and brother and knew right from the start that I wanted to be a goalie.

My very first year of hockey (1978).

In 1979–80, I played in the Los Angeles Forum. Thirteen years later, my first NHL win would be in the same building, against Wayne Gretzky and the LA Kings.

In 1972, I was selected for the Calgary All-Star team.

My grade nine graduation, sporting the Don Johnson look.

In net for Team Pacific at the Canadian U-16 championships held in Calgary. Michael Stewart (*right*) was also drafted by the New York Rangers, and we played together on the Calgary All-Star team and again in the minors in Binghamton.

In the Alberta Junior Hockey League (1987–88), I was one of a handful of goalies to play Junior A as a 15-year-old.

Signing my Western Hockey League contract with the Kamloops Blazers.

My first Western Hockey League game with the Kamloops Blazers. We won 4–1 against the Tri-City Americans.

Winning the Memorial Cup in Seattle in my last season (1992). It was the first Memorial Cup win for the Kamloops Blazers, and we won in the last 15 seconds of the game.

With the Memorial Cup. Darryl Sydor (*left*) went on to win two Stanley Cups.

My first NHL call-up in 1992, and the first time I skated on the ice at Madison Square Garden. My dad took this photo. In the background (*top, centre*), you can see Mike Richter, who I wanted to be like. He is probably the hardest-working goalie I've ever seen.

My first-ever start at Madison Square Garden, against Mario Lemieux and the Penguins. Mario had three goals on me. BRUCE BENNETT/GETTY IMAGES

At the Miss Teen USA competition in 1993. Playing for the New York Rangers is like playing for the Yankees in that you get invited to many events. Kennedy Montgomery (*in black, fifth from right*) was an MTV VJ, and she became a very close friend during my time with the Rangers.

My first NHL rookie card. Every kid dreams of winning a Stanley Cup and having a hockey card.

My first-ever game in Calgary's Saddle-dome, which was special for me because I was a huge Calgary Flames fan as a kid. I grew up in Calgary and always dreamt of playing in that building.

At the 1994 Olympics in Lillehammer, Norway. These Olympics were the last time I can remember feeling free of OCD.

Proud parents. Some neighbours got this lawn sign for my mom and dad just before the last game of the Olympics.

The gold-winning goal in the shootout at the Lillehammer Olympics. I was literally an inch away from winning a gold medal. DON EMMERT/AFP/GETTY IMAGES

The Swedish postal service issued a stamp to commemorate Forsberg's goal.

My pads from the Olympic Games are in the Hockey Hall of Fame. It was the first time a custom-made logo appeared on a pair of goalie pads. Together they form the Canadian flag.

HOCKEY HALL OF FAME AND MUSEUM

Celebrating my first year as a professional hockey player in the summer of 1993 with my dad and brother.

With the Stanley Cup in 1994. Despite achieving my dream of holding the Cup, I was struggling so much with my mental health that I didn't stay in New York for the Stanley Cup parade.

Wearing the alternate jersey in my first year with the Canucks. Adrian Aucoin is the defenceman behind me. Adrian played in the Olympics and was one of my best friends throughout my time in Vancouver.

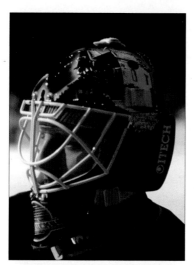

As a kid, I loved scary goalie masks. In my first year with the Vancouver Canucks, their black, yellow and blood-red jerseys inspired my *Psycho* mask, which featured Alfred Hitchcock and the Bates Motel. It became an iconic mask and is now in the Hockey Hall of Fame.

Presenting my *Psycho* mask to Craig Campbell at the Hockey Hall of Fame.

My second year in Vancouver. That was the year I reached out to get help and saved my own life by doing so. DENIS BRODEUR/NHLI VIA GETTY IMAGES

The game puck from my first NHL shutout against Boston. It's one of the infamous Fox-Trax glowing pucks.

Coaching Jordan Binnington of the St. Louis Blues. Jordan went on to help the Blues win the Stanley Cup in 2019.

The Joe Louis Arena in Detroit. My son, Hayden, played in a hockey tournament at this arena, the same one where I had my first NHL start. An incredible moment to appreciate my journey. iStock by Getty Images

Fostering mental health takes a village.

Never be afraid to reach out for help when you need it.
My "village" includes some of my best friends. I lean on them,
and they always check in to see if I'm okay.

Clint Malarchuk, an NHL All-Star and a mental health mentor for me.

Hiking in Scottsdale, Arizona, with Rob Cowie. Rob played for the Los Angeles Kings and is now a scout for the Nashville Predators.

Former NHL players and two of my best friends, Jeff Sharples (*left*) and Rod Buskas (*right*). They are both professional pilots now.

Going golfing with Jeff Stipec, the former Vancouver Canucks COO, who is a mentor and good friend.

More of my posse of best friends: Sean Burke (*left*) and Russ Courtnall (*right*), also former NHL players.

At my mom and dad's 50th anniversary. Emphatic, funny and kind, my mom has always been in my corner.

The most important people in my life: my kids, Alexa, Hayden and Farrah. I couldn't be more proud of the people they've become.

time for me. Obviously, by that time, everyone knew there was "something going on with Hirschey." They saw me wither into a husk before their eyes over the course of a season. They saw me lying basically in the fetal position in the locker room. They saw me have an out-of-body experience during a practice. They knew that I was really suffering. But my silence opened the door for them to create their own interpretation of what was happening, and it was completely the opposite of what was true. There were always whispers of what was wrong with me, but no one really knew anything. Drugs. Alcohol. Women. Whatever. I was withdrawing and fighting my OCD most days, not wanting anyone to think I was weak. So guys drew their own conclusions.

A third of the guys thought I was a piece of shit and wanted me gone.

A third of guys were really empathetic and tried to reach out.

And a third of guys were just indifferent.

A lot of days in that locker room, I felt like I had the plague. Not many guys wanted to hang out with me. I lost a lot of friends. All the excuses, the hiding, and being late for things had taken their toll. On road trips, it seemed like no one wanted to go out to dinner with me anymore. I got used to eating alone, or just staying in my hotel room. The one guy who always tried to look out for me was Dave Babych. Dave would often see that I was alone and ask if I wanted to go get some dinner with him. (Thank you from the bottom of my heart, Dave.)

A few teammates actually had gone to Pat Quinn asking him to trade me because they said that I was a bad teammate. That hurt, but I never held any ill will towards those who did that. I knew they didn't understand. I mean, just to give you an idea of how eccentric my behaviour probably seemed, and the steps I was taking to hide what I was dealing with, I remember this one time before we played St. Louis, I was in net that night, and I really freaking out before the game. I actually ran out of the locker room as we were getting dressed and went to the pay phone in the hallway so I could call my therapist to calm me down.

It's a half an hour before the game, and I'm on the pay phone, and the coaches are walking by, the training staff are walking by. Nobody has any idea what's going on with me, so they just assume that I'm talking to my girlfriend or God knows who else—my agent, my drug dealer? Everybody just thinks I'm an asshole. But in reality I have my hand cupped over the phone and I'm whispering to my therapist that my anxiety is through the roof and I can't calm my thoughts down. Coaches are literally walking by looking at me and mouthing, "Hirschey? Hirschey, what the *fuck*?"

The funniest part is that my therapist *did* calm me down, and I ended up going out that night and stopping 42 shots in a shutout.

A few weeks later against the Kings, the same thing happened, but when I rang up my therapist he didn't pick up. I couldn't stop my meltdown, and I went out that night and had a nightmare in net.

That's when the pills started. After three months of treatment, I was still having a rough go of it. I was starting to spiral again, so I asked my psychologist if there was anything more we could do to balance me out. The talk therapy was not working. He assigned me to a psychiatrist—a doctor who put me on a medication called Zoloft. The medication took time to reach its full effect, so the process was painfully slow. The psychiatrist then added what's called an antipsychotic medication to my Zoloft to see if that could kick-start things. Boy, was that a bad idea. I tried to play in Ottawa on them, and it was disastrous. I went to make a save in the first period where the puck hit my chest and dropped down to my feet. I went to cover it, but I saw three pucks. I put my hand down and completely missed the real puck, and a Senator player buried the rebound. We were down 3–0 before I could blink. After the fifth goal, they pulled me. Sometimes I wonder what would've happened if I had told everybody the truth. Just gathered all the reporters around my locker and let it fly.

"Hirschey, what the hell happened out there tonight?"

"Well, I have a mental health disorder and I'm on Zoloft and antipsychotics and I haven't slept in three days, and I was on the phone with my therapist before the game because I'm still obsessed with the crippling thought that I'm going to give everyone I've ever known and loved HIV, and to be honest I was seeing three pucks out there tonight. But the boys played hard!"

I battled every day for the rest of the season. In March, management was trying desperately to shake up the team and reach the playoffs. Esa Tikkanen and Russ Courtnall were traded to the New York Rangers for Sergei Nemchinov and Brian Noonan. We only lost once in the last 10 games, but it was too little, too late. We missed the playoffs for the first time in seven seasons.

The season mercifully ended, and I was emotionally and mentally spent. It was the longest year of my life. Each day I was taking two steps forward and one step back.

But you know what? I was *alive*. I was still here.

Reaching out for help that day in New Jersey was the best thing I ever did. It was more important than any save I'd ever made on the ice. I knew deep down that I had saved my own life.

10

After hitting rock bottom in front of all my teammates, I needed to get away from Vancouver that summer of 1997. I was exhausted and needed to recharge, so my girlfriend and I spent the summer in Malibu, soaking up the sun on the beach and getting away from hockey. I spent the time healing and sometimes went golfing at Sherwood Golf and Country Club with Russ Courtnall or Alex Mogilny, who also lived in Malibu. It was the perfect spot for me to get better. We rented a one-bedroom loft overlooking the ocean and listened to the waves crash on the beach while falling asleep every night. It was peaceful and serene—exactly what I needed. I studied meditation, took a martial arts class and focused on healing. Unfortunately, with things going well, I let my guard down a bit and didn't get therapy on a regular basis, which was a mistake. The cold hard fact is that I needed therapy for OCD and was going to for the rest of my life. That's just the way it is, but I thought I was better and didn't need it anymore.

After that debacle of a season, I'm certain that Vancouver had no idea what to do with me. I should have communicated immediately what I was diagnosed with. I should have told my teammates, but I was afraid. The stigma was real, and the perception was that mental illness meant weakness, which is the furthest thing from the truth. I was on a one-way contract, so I was hoping I was safe. Pat Quinn was a great man, but he and the coaching staff had never before seen anything like what I went through. I'm sure they saw me as damaged goods and a problem, just like the Rangers did. Just like any team would have, back then.

They were making big changes everywhere. In July, they signed Mark Messier to a three-year deal. Mess was a great leader and was captain when the Rangers won the Stanley Cup in 1994, and going back to 1990, he was captain when the Edmonton Oilers won the Cup. I was jacked. I played with Mess in New York and thought it was going to be a great addition. After all, I witnessed the man lead the Rangers to the Stanley Cup in New York City. The pressure was immense, and this guy did what no one else could in 54 years. He has his detractors, but I don't care what anyone says—Mess was good to me.

In August, I was getting ready for the upcoming season when the Canucks announced they had signed Arturs Irbe as a free agent. I was stunned. What was the team doing? I was now in a three-way battle to play in Vancouver—Kirk McLean, me and Arturs Irbe. My agent called the Canucks and asked about the situation and was told that the best two goalies out of training camp were going to make the team and that the other guy would be traded.

So I went to camp still hiding my illness, pretending like nothing had happened the previous year, and I actually had a great training camp. I thought for sure I was safe. I looked

THE SAVE OF MY LIFE

forward to going with the Canucks to Japan for the preseason. It was the first time in NHL history that the season was going to begin with two teams playing regular season games outside of North America. The Canucks and the Mighty Ducks of Anaheim were selected as the two teams, and we'd play a two-game series in Tokyo. The idea was that the games would attract attention to hockey in advance of the 1998 Winter Olympics to be held in Nagano.

When we got to Japan, it was immediately apparent that I was the odd man out. I was the third goalie from the get-go. I didn't play. In fact, I never even dressed. That's when I figured out that I wasn't making the team. I was starting to get concerned about being buried in the minors, and never seeing NHL ice again, after everything that happened. Maybe the word was out that I had been diagnosed with something. I was so paranoid.

I watched both games from the stands and called my agent to start talking to teams to try to get me out of there. My agent had no luck finding a trading partner, so when the team got back from Japan, I was put on waivers. Simply put, waivers are when every other NHL team gets a free opportunity to claim a player for nothing. All they have to do is pick up his contract.

No one wanted me.

I was going back to the minors, again. It felt like my dream was dead.

It's obvious why they waived me, but if you just went by my play on the ice, I should have been given a chance. Honestly, at the time, I still hadn't grasped the magnitude of what happened the year prior. I self-destructed in front of my teammates. It was scary for them to watch that happen to a person. I'm sure that even the guys who did care about me were probably thinking, *Should this guy really be in an NHL locker room right now?*

They didn't know what was wrong with me, and I didn't do anything to help them empathize with me or connect in any way. I was just totally shut down and paranoid. It was a lesson to be learned that when struggling with mental health, communication to those around me was important. Hiding it only created more shame, disgust, embarrassment and problems. Does that mean I needed to tell everyone my business? Definitely not, but leaving things open to interpretation, like I did, only lets people's imaginations run wild. On the outside, it looked as though

I didn't care when, in fact, I cared too much what everyone thought of me. I wasn't a bad guy. I was suffering. But unfortunately, I let the stigma win, and I stayed silent. I didn't want to ruin my career, so I ruined my career.

When I was first put on waivers, my agent actually heard that the Phoenix Coyotes were going to claim me. I liked that prospect—a new start in a place with nice hot weather. But the waiver deadline came and went with no call from the Coyotes. They passed on me and picked up Jimmy Waite from the Chicago Blackhawks. In retrospect, I have to suspect that the Coyotes did some research on me and heard through the grapevine that I had some off-ice issues, but I'll never know for sure.

Since I wasn't claimed, the Canucks sent me down to their minor league team in Syracuse. It was humbling, to say the least. I was tired. Tired of running from my own brain and also tired from chasing the NHL dream. I sat at home for a week, thinking that I might just quit and give up on the only dream I'd had since I was seven years old. The burden of my illness and of the roller coaster of my recovery process was so heavy, and I'd been hiding the truth every single day of my life. Now I had to adjust to yet another new environment in Syracuse—a new locker room, new teammates, new lies I'd have to invent. It felt like the walls were closing in on me.

The last thing I wanted to do was give up on hockey. But I was just so damn tired. I needed a shot of energy. I needed a purpose. I needed a miracle. And that's when my girlfriend and I got the greatest news of our lives. In my lowest moment, when I wanted to give up, I found out I was going to be a father.

She was pregnant with our first child. I was really going to be a dad.

The problem with writing a book is that so many things about mental health are hard to put into words. You struggle to convey what they haven't invented words for yet. For sounds, feelings, emotions, rage, shame, anger. But if it's hard to find the words for mental health, then finding the words for that moment when you find out that you're going to be a father?

Well, that's impossible. I won't even try. I'll just say that it was the miracle that I needed to keep going—not just in hockey, but in life. I decided to report to Syracuse and give it my best shot. I was going to be a minor league goalie for most of that season, and I knew it. But the ice is the ice. As soon as I got out there, and I could focus on stopping that little black puck, all the voices in my head went away, and everything went silent again, and I could focus all my obsessions and fear and anxiety and anger and loneliness and rage and pain into one thing.

Stop the puck.

Horse blinders.

Nothing else exists.

Stillness.

Peace in the chaos.

Stop the puck, stop the puck, winger coming down the left side with speed, right-handed shot, dangerdangerdangerdanger, come out of the crease cut the angle down take his space away, he's slowing down getting ready to shoot but watch the back door if he passes dangerdangerDANGER his eyes just glanced up he's shooting he's SHOOTING get ready, don't drop down too early, don't drop don't drop don't drop, wait, wait, wait, SHOT, track it, track it, puck hit your chest, REBOUND REBOUND REBOUND whereisit whereisit wherewherewhere, black spot in the corner of your eyes— there it is THERE IT IS. COVER COVER COVER COVER IT.

Whistle. Frozen. Safe. We're safe we're safe we're safe. Okay. Okay.

"Nice stop, Hirschey."

Safe. Safe. Safe.

Complete focus, in 20-minute chunks. My sanctuary.

Off the ice, I was still very shaky. During that season, because I hadn't had enough therapy to that point, the embarrassment and shame would still creep in. I caught myself wondering what others thought of me, whether they knew the story. I heard the whispers, I knew there was talk behind my back, but there was nothing I could do. I left a lot of damage in my wake and it was going to take a long time to repair friendships that suffered while I was hiding a mental illness.

I'll never forget one time when I was feeling sorry for myself for being down in the minors, and my coach, Jack McIlhargey, a former Vancouver Canuck, noticed I was pouting about it. Jack pulled me aside and said, "Hirschey, no one feels sorry for you. The only way out of the AHL is to play your way out."

He was right. It was hard to hear, but it was what I needed. I used that advice often over the years, and not just in hockey. The only way out of my mental health issues was to *do the work*.

No one was going to do it for me. At that point, I was relying too much on my medication to get me through the days, and I wasn't keeping up with my therapy sessions. I wasn't doing the hard part. I can tell you from my own experience that medication is great. It's essential. But you're not going to find all the answers in the bottom of a pill bottle.

After Jack's talk with me, I started refocusing on my recovery, and after a few months, I felt good about my game, my life, and we had a baby on the way. So right before Christmas, I took my girlfriend to New York City. We walked to see the big Christmas tree in Rockefeller Center, and I got down on one knee and proposed to her.

She said yes.

It's kind of incredible to me, in retrospect, because four years prior to that moment, in that very same city, I was at the top of the Empire State Building, telling my mother that I just wanted to die. Now I was getting married, and I was going to be a father, and I was able to have nights—not every night, but a lot of nights—where I could lay my head on my pillow and feel at peace.

The only reason I was able to experience that transformation is because I said three magic words: "I need help."

Now, what would be great for this book is if I could tell you that, after all that, the Canucks called me back up to the team and I helped them go on a run to the Stanley Cup Final with Bure and Bertuzzi and Messier.

Yeah. That didn't happen.

I got called up for one game that season. December 31. Philadelphia. I was the backup. I thought I was going to sit on the bench for two hours, grab a shower and then be sent back down to the minors. But the Flyers came out and lit us up for three goals in the first 11 minutes. I'm sitting there thinking, *Please, please, please. Put me in.* I was itching for a chance to play an NHL game again. Sure enough, Mike Keenan came over and gave me the tap on the shoulder. I was going in. After half a season in the minors, I was back, baby. I was going to show them that I belonged in the net. I got my chance.

Hell, I wish I'd have stayed on the bench! It was a nightmare. A *shitshow*, as we say. The Flyers just kept rolling. They put five past me after Irbe got yanked, and although I didn't play that badly, when you're the goalie, nobody cares. All that matters is what's on the scoreboard. We got embarrassed in our own building. Things got violent, as they usually did in those circumstances back in the day. Eight different fights, four misconducts, blood on the ice, pandemonium. When the horn mercifully sounded, the game finished 8–0. It became known as the New Year's Eve Massacre, and looking back, it's almost poetic that I was the one in the net in my *Psycho* mask that night. It was certainly a bloodbath.

I never saw an NHL locker room again that season. And you know what? I'm extremely proud of that year, despite it being such a low point in my career. I went back to Syracuse and finished the season, and we ended up finishing third in our division and made the playoffs. We lost to the Hamilton Bulldogs in the first round of the playoffs, but I did all I could. I was dealing with everything that life could possibly throw my way, but I kept putting on my gear every night. I kept going out there. I didn't quit.

That summer, I got the best gift of all. On June 18, my beautiful daughter was born. I never knew my capacity to love could be so deep. I had spent so many years in such a dark spiral of fear and shame and anxiety and loneliness, thinking that I wasn't worthy of love. Thinking that I would never have a family. Thinking that I was insane. Thinking that I didn't want to exist. Thinking that I was a monster, frankly.

And now I had this beautiful soul in my arms, and I realized how wrong all of that was. It was the indisputable proof that my brain was lying to me. It was more powerful, honestly, than anything that a therapist could tell me. The love that I felt when I held her was immeasurable, and would have seemed impossible to me when I was just a lost soul, sitting in my car, looking out over that cliff, convinced that I should end my life.

It gives me chills to think about now. It's the reason why I am sharing my story in such painful detail. Because I know how many people out there are suffering right now, thinking that it's never going to change. Thinking that they're broken. Thinking that they will never experience love like that.

And all I can say to you is: I *was* you.

If I didn't get help, I would have missed out on the birth of my children. I would have missed lacing up my son's skates for the first time. I would have missed listening to my oldest daughter's beautiful voice when she plays her guitar. I would have missed seeing my youngest daughter prance onstage in *The Nutcracker*. I would have missed her waving to me in the crowd. All those wonderful things . . . gone.

But I got help. It was a hell hike up that mountain over the years. It was gruelling. It was embarrassing. It was not simple. But I got help. Eventually, I found a lot of joy, even in the small things in life.

If you are in a dark place right now, thinking that you can't go on anymore, I know you probably cannot foresee these kinds of things in your future. But your brain is lying to you. It's lying. Just hang on a little longer. Just keep going. Just say the three magic words: I need help.

11

Over the next five seasons after the birth of my daughter, I played a grand total of 23 NHL games. Mostly, I was a minor league goalie. And I was *everywhere*. Syracuse, Utah, Milwaukee, Cincinnati, Albany, Portland, Philly, back to Utah. Everywhere.

It wasn't that I was blackballed or anything like that. It was a combination of things. The new butterfly style of goaltending was becoming dominant, and it was vastly more effective than the stand-up style I played. Teams started moving towards taller goalies, and it made sense—a bigger goalie covers more net. I was getting pushed out for those reasons, and I was for-ever fighting the stigma of my reputation from when I was sick. People still didn't know about my OCD or the medication I was on, so I can understand. But I wasn't exactly known as a "good chemistry guy," let's put it that way.

The thing is, my dreams had changed. My wife got preg-nant with our second child in 1999, and by that point, my priorities were totally recalibrated towards my family. I still badly wanted to be an NHL goalie, but there wasn't the same crushing expectation and anxiety that surrounded it when I was a 22-year-old kid. It was a means of providing for my family and giving them a good life. Our son was born on March 16, 2000, in Salt Lake City. We never knew the sexes of our children before their births, so when my son arrived and the doctor told us it was a boy, it felt like getting the greatest surprise gift ever. Holding him in my arms for the first time was a revelation. Nothing in life can compare to it. I had the perfect family—a boy and a girl. I was relatively healthy, at least I thought I was, and other than not being in the NHL, I was in a good place and at peace.

For the next three years, I was in the most stable place that I'd ever been in. There were even days when I felt like, *Hey, maybe I have this thing beat. Maybe this nightmare is all over.* And that's the tricky thing about mental health, and that's especially the tricky thing about OCD. It's never over. It can be in control. It can be managed. You can live an amazing and healthy life. But you can never tell yourself that you've got it beat.

For me, every time I start getting cocky, my illness tends to humble me.

In March 2003, I had a relapse. It was bad. I was playing in the NHL for the Dallas Stars at the time. Marty Turco had gotten hurt, so I got called up to back up Ron Tugnutt. I kind of knew that it was the end of the road for me in the NHL—probably my last shot to show the league that I had my shit together and I could be a dependable backup. So I'm sure I had some anxiety building up under the surface that I wasn't addressing.

Then Edmonton happened.

Every player, every goalie—hell, every athlete—has an arena that just seems cursed for them. For me, it was always Edmonton. The ice was hard, it was cold, and it felt like the players seemed to be able to shoot the puck harder and skate faster in that barn. The Oilers were my kryptonite. Out of five or six starts in Edmonton, I'd only had one good game.

Game day came, and I was in net. Since we could see the writing on the wall, my parents drove up to watch me. I didn't sleep the afternoon of the game, because I knew that if I didn't play well, that would be it. My NHL career would be done. It felt a little bit like the bad old days in the locker room before the game. I couldn't get my anxiety under control. I was shaky. I wanted to run out of the room. But I did my routine and I held it all together.

The game started, and fortunately I was able to lock in. I got through the first period not allowing a goal. I was feeling good. Edmonton came out and scored two quick goals in the second, but I was still in control and playing well. After two periods, the game was knotted at 2–2. Then, halfway through the third, the unthinkable happened.

Edmonton dumped the puck into our end, and I collected the puck behind my net, and I went to pass it up the boards to our winger. It's something that happens 20 times every game. But unfortunately for me, Derian Hatcher, my own defenceman, was backtracking to pick the puck up from me. I didn't see him coming, and with our lack of communication, I fired it directly into his shin pads. The puck bounced right onto the stick of the Oilers' Shawn Horcoff in the slot. I was stuck behind the net. Helpless. He had a tap-in for a goal into an empty net. It's the stuff you see in your nightmares, as a goalie.

Right then, in the moment, I knew it was over. I knew it was done. Even if we came back to win, it was a mistake that couldn't be made by a veteran goalie. I wasn't going to get another chance to play in the National Hockey League. After the game, I saw my mom and dad, and I wasn't even devastated. I was calm. If that was going to be my last NHL game, at least my parents got to see it.

I had done so much work on myself that I didn't go off the rails. It's like my anxiety and sadness were a person sitting in the room with me, and I could acknowledge them, but they weren't me. The dream was coming to an end, and that was okay. Sad, but okay. It was a good run. But then after that game, things went from bad to worse because of a freak accident. We were back in Dallas, and I was in the locker room fixing my goalie pads with a sharp blade when it slipped and gashed my leg. The cut was deep and there was blood everywhere. My immediate thought was, *Holy shit, what if someone before me used the blade and they cut themselves and the blade is tainted with HIV?*

It didn't make any rational sense. It was an absurd thought. But OCD doesn't care. If doesn't care what's rational. It doesn't care how much therapy you've had. It doesn't matter if you're in a good place. It doesn't matter if you've got a kids at home and a happy family and a good life. It's brutal. It's unpredictable. It's back. It's back with a vengeance now for me.

Back back back back dark dark dark dark dark HIV HIV HIV you'll give it to your kids you're going to hurt them dark dark dark dark you have it YOU HAVE IT YOU HAVE IT THEY WILL HAVE IT THEY WILL HAVE IT YOU ARE GOING TO KILL THEM WITH THIS DISEASE HIV HIV HIV DARKDARK-DARKDARKDARKDARKDARK.

Full volume. Relentless. Screaming at me.

I hid it from everyone and functioned as best I could. I was sent back to the minors in Utah and finished the season there with my OCD in full tilt. I didn't talk to my wife about it, as we were having enough issues already. We had communication problems, as she was tired of the OCD issues and of the grind of the hockey lifestyle and the toll it took on our family. I didn't want her thinking anything was wrong with me. I didn't want to add to the pile that I had been triggered again and was obsessed with the thought that I was going to hurt our children. In my mind, I was the man of the family, and I felt I couldn't even talk to her about it. (A mistake, for sure, but it was nearly impossible to hear my own rational thoughts, with how loud the voices were in my head.)

This is one of the hardest things in this whole book for me to admit, but I need to say it for those out there who can relate to it, who probably think they're the only one . . .

At that point, I was so convinced that I had HIV that hugging my own kids would send me spinning for hours. I didn't want to touch anyone. I didn't want to see anyone. I felt like I was a monster. Like always, somewhere deep in my subconscious, I *knew* the truth. I knew I didn't have HIV, but the chaos and confusion in my brain made it difficult to sort through. The years of not getting enough therapy, thinking I was out of the woods and relying only on medication, really bit me in the ass.

It's one thing when the object of your obsessive thoughts is you, or your girlfriend, or your wife. But when it's your *kids*? When it's your own children, the light of your life, it's absolutely unbearable. My OCD has this incredible knack of slithering sideways, waiting in the weeds and pouncing on something else when I least expect it. This time, it morphed into whatever it felt would hurt me the most. It preyed on the fact that I loved my family more than anything. It convinced me that they were going to get sick and die, and it was going to be all my fault.

Thank God, right around this time, I got another lifeline.

It had been six years since my diagnosis, and I was so tired of my OCD. I just wanted it to go away. Having an OCD attack is like living life with everything around you on fire. It's bloody exhausting. I knew that whatever I was doing wasn't enough anymore, and that I needed more professional help. So I went online and did a bunch of research, and I found this clinic in Los Angeles called OCDLA. I called the founder, and he asked me what I was dealing with. I told him that I didn't have physical compulsions like hand washing. Then I was about to go on, and he stopped me mid-sentence and out of the blue he asked me, "Harm thoughts? Religious or sexually intrusive? Which do you deal with?"

I went silent. The light bulb went off. No one had phrased it like that to me before. This guy knew exactly what I was going through. He told me I most likely had what's called Pure-O. It's a version of OCD that has an extremely subtle but extremely important difference. Unlike people with germ OCD who compulsively wash their hands to relieve anxiety, everything I did was in my head, and no one else could see it. It's actually how I was able to hide my OCD for so many years in the locker room and in front of TV cameras. I didn't have all those physical compulsions that would have been a dead giveaway. You didn't see me flick the lights 10 times when I came into the locker room or repeat the same word 15 times in a row or obsessively tape my stick over and over. All of those obsessions and tics were happening, but they were happening in my brain, at 200 miles an hour, invisible to the naked eye.

The doctor explained to me Pure-O is classified in three different categories: harm thoughts, religious thoughts, and sexually intrusive thoughts. I'd had experience with all three. It was a revelation.

We were living in Las Vegas at the time, so throughout that summer, I made the five-hour drive to LA for therapy four or five times. We were just getting started, and I was learning a lot about my OCD, when I stopped into a blood donor drive at a clinic in Las Vegas. When you give blood, it's protocol that they test it for HIV, and so without even realizing it, I'd had an HIV test. I know that for the average person, it seems really odd that I didn't just get regular HIV tests over the years to relieve my anxiety. Well, the thing is, that's what someone thinking rationally would do.

I think I may have a tooth infection.

Okay, I'll go to the dentist and see.

Oh, hey, look, I don't have a tooth infection.

But that's not how someone's brain works when they have Pure-O. In my mind, there was no reason to even work up the strength to go get an HIV test, because there was nothing to discover. I *had* HIV. Period. It's in my blood. It's there. Why get a test? In fact, the only thing to discover was who gave it to me. The only thing to obsess over was how to protect my family from contracting it. *It's there. It's inside me. It's over. There's nothing to test. In fact, even if I got a test and the test came back negative, then the test is lying. There's a mistake. They're purposely lying to you, and you'll let your guard down and give HIV to everyone you know.*

Do you see how this terrible cycle works?

So I spent years never getting an HIV test, despite HIV being a relentless fear. After years of therapy, and after discovering that I had Pure-O, when I was finally in a stable enough place to donate blood at the blood drive in Las Vegas, my bloodwork came back from the clinic with a negative HIV test result. Just like that, almost with a snap of a finger, my OCD immediately ceased, and my HIV thoughts completely disappeared. I felt a flush go through my body—a grip that let go. With that test, suddenly there was nothing for my OCD to latch on to.

Naively, I thought that maybe it was over. Maybe that was the final hurdle, and I had finally solved my OCD. Around that time, life got hectic. So I stopped making the five-hour drive to

LA for therapy. It was just too much of a commute, and I had to worry about my livelihood. I had to stay on the roller coaster of pro hockey for as long as I could. With my NHL career winding down, it was time for Europe. I spent the next three seasons playing overseas in Germany and Sweden, trying to squirrel away as much money as I could for my family before the wheels came off and I had to retire. I had two kids at home, and then when I was playing overseas in 2004, we got another surprise. We were going to have our third child. That's a lot of college tuition! I was just praying that my knees were going to hold up. When you're a 32-year-old goalie playing overseas, the mission is very simple: just keep getting those cheques, old man!

I was playing for a team in Kassel, Germany, at the time, and what a disaster that was! The owner was in the process of selling the team, and the coach who brought me there got fired after five games. The owner stopped buying the players new sticks and hired the coach from the peewee team to coach us. The only English he knew was swear words, and it was so bad that one of our players, Mark Greig, coached our power play. I thought I'd seen it all in this game. It was so surreal that it was almost funny.

With a child on the way, I just kept my mouth shut and tried to enjoy it for what it was. It was still hockey, sort of.

My wife was nervous about giving birth overseas, and I don't blame her. In late February, she started having contractions, so off we went to the hospital. The doctor met us there, and after a few hours, he told us that the baby wasn't ready and that we should go home and wait it out. I didn't feel right about that from the moment he said it. It was something in my gut. I knew that with my wife's earlier pregnancies, she'd had trouble dilating and had to be induced. I started arguing with the doctor and demanded that she be dilated immediately. I was adamant that we were not leaving. He reluctantly agreed. I was in the room for the birth, and I noticed something wasn't right. My daughter arrived, but the nurse immediately grabbed her and ran with her to another room. I knew something was terribly wrong. That doesn't happen in the TV shows unless the baby is dying. I was stunned. What the hell just happened?

I looked at my wife. She was exhausted and spent from pushing, and she was looking to me for answers. I ran out of the room, and I could see a number of nurses and doctors way down the hall, gathered around the baby in another room. I couldn't breathe. I was terrified. I ran down the hall, and as I got closer, I could see a tiny oxygen mask held up to her face. The nurse was pumping the small yellow bulb to try to force oxygen into her lungs. I was about to throw up. It was all happening so fast and so slow at the same time. Everything was silent. I thought I was going to pass out. Then all of a sudden . . .

I heard the nurse clap and scream in elation.

"She's breathing! She's breathing!"

Our baby girl was alive. She was okay.

She was breathing. She was breathing. She was breathing.

Our baby girl was breathing.

I had spent so much of my life obsessing and worrying and trying to control everything. And of course, in a moment, everything was taken out of my hands. The most precious thing in the world, our daughter, was in the hands of fate. It was an extremely humbling and eye-opening experience.

It turned out that she was born with the umbilical cord wrapped around her neck. If we had gone home like the doctor wanted us to, and if I had not been adamant about my wife being induced, there is no doubt that she would not have made it. I do not blame the doctor. He was only doing what he knew. But I commend that nurse who sprang into action. She saved my daughter's life. For that, I am eternally grateful.

When that season ended, I knew I probably only had one more year left in the tank. Retirement was looming, I only had a high school education, and I was terrified of what the future held. I had some money saved, but by no means was I going to be able to retire and do nothing the rest of my life. I would have to find a job, and all I knew was hockey.

I spent what I knew would be my final season in Malmö, Sweden, with the Redhawks. I absolutely loved it. If you're an old pro looking for one last great ride, I can't recommend Sweden highly enough. Malmö is located across the bridge from Copenhagen, Denmark, and its weather is mild, similar to Vancouver's. The people are amazing, and I made some good friends. My kids went to school in Malmö and in my opinion, Sweden did education right. School was about the kids. They got plenty of love and support from teachers and programs. I was so happy there that if I was told I had to live there for the rest of my life and never leave,

I would have been 100 percent fine with it. My eldest daughter learned Swedish quickly and blended right in.

It was the perfect way to end my hockey career. I had a terrific season, earning 10 shutouts, and my goals-against average was just over 1.60. Over there, the top four teams in the second-tier league play a qualification series against the bottom two teams in the Elite League. It's a promotion-and-relegation system, like international soccer. We won the qualification round, and Malmö won promotion into the Elite League, which is almost as cool as winning a championship, because it changes the fortune of an entire team and town. It was awesome.

I retired after that final game in Sweden. It was the perfect way for me to end my playing career, in a place that I loved, surrounded by my family. I was officially done, and I never looked back. I had no desire to ever play goalie again. But I also knew how hard it can be for pro athletes to walk away and start their second life. Especially athletes with mental health issues.

I was 33. I had three kids and an entire life in front of me. Now what the hell was I going to *do* with it? I knew one thing for sure. I couldn't sit at home alone with my brain all day.

That was a recipe for disaster. I had to find a purpose. I had to find my next path. As any former professional athlete will tell you . . . it ain't easy. That road can take you down a lot of dark and strange places.

As a matter of fact, a couple years later, I would find myself thrown into the back of an unmarked van on the back streets of Moscow, getting screamed at by five very scary-looking Russian gangsters, thinking that I was going to need Liam Neeson to come save me.

Yes, believe it or not, before I was able to find the light, things somehow got a little bit darker.

12

didn't know what the hell I wanted to be. I looked into being a pilot, a police officer and a firefighter, although my OCD and fear of HIV and blood ended my chances of being a firefighter. I wasn't a US citizen at the time, so I couldn't be a cop. I was lost. Then I got this call that changed the direction of my life.

When I was playing, I always wore Vaughn goaltending equipment. Every summer, before the next season started, the Vaughn rep would call me and ask me what I needed for equipment. Living the dream, right? Well, this time, when I was retired, the phone call went a little different. The rep could tell I was a bit lost and feeling sorry for myself. That's when he said the words I won't ever forget. He said, "Hirschey, no one is looking out for you anymore. You aren't a hockey player. Nobody is asking what Corey Hirsch is doing. You're going to have to let people know that you're out there and available to work."

It hurt, but it hit home. It reminded me a lot of what my coach in Syracuse told me, all those years ago. No one was coming to save me. I had to do the work. I'd had everything taken care of for me from the time I was 16 years old. I'd always had a team that made a schedule, telling me where I needed to be and when. I always had a coach who ran practices and made the drills. All I had to do was show up. I had billets in junior who cooked and cleaned for me, and an agent who got me jobs with teams when I was a pro. Now I had to do it on my own. No one else was going to call and offer me a new career. I had to do it.

Armed with that advice, I called Brad Pascall and Scott Salmond, two VPs with the men's programs at Hockey Canada, to set up a meeting in Calgary. I knew it was a long shot. I went into the Hockey Canada office in Calgary, and it just so happened that Ian Clark, who had been the goaltending con-sultant the previous season, had been hired to be a goalie coach with the Vancouver Canucks. Brad looked at me and said, "Our goalie consultant just left. Do you want to watch our World Junior goalies at summer camp and give us your opinion?"

Heck yeah I did.

And that's how my next career began. Pure luck and timing. I was basically an unpaid intern at the age of 33. I scouted their goalies for free, turned in my reports, and they were an instant hit within the organization. I took it a step further in early Sep-tember 2006. I proposed a role as the first-ever full-time goal-tending consultant for Hockey Canada, a role they'd never had before. I would travel across Canada scouting young goalies for Hockey Canada amateur teams, forge a relationship, then coach them if they made a Hockey Canada team. Scott and Brad liked the idea, and I agreed to a salary of $3,000 Canadian a month with no benefits just to get my foot in the door. I could live and travel out of Las Vegas. To put my salary in perspective, my first contract in my first year as a pro at the age of 20 paid me $32,500 US playing in the minors. The contract I had just signed with Hockey Canada was less than what I had made as a 20-year-old.

I was starting at the beginning again.

The first year was fantastic. I found a real love for scouting and coaching. I'll be honest, I was clueless about the hours and time I would have to put into a workday post-hockey. I had been done with practice and out for lunch every day by noon for the last 13 years. One of the biggest complaints I had heard from teams that hire former players is that they have no clue how to work a full day. Coaching is a 15-hour commitment every day. The reality of scouting is travelling and watching 200 games a year. But the structure helped me a lot, and mentally, I was doing well again. I found new satisfaction in helping others. In the two years as goalie coach with Hockey Canada, we won back-to-back gold medals at the World Junior Champion-ships—the first with Carey Price in 2007 and then the second in 2008 with Steve Mason. As a former player and now a coach, it gave me a medal from every World Championship hockey event possible, which is very cool and very rare.

I hadn't had any OCD flare-ups in almost three years. I really

THE SAVE OF MY LIFE

thought I had kicked my OCD. I had even stopped taking my medication. Life was headed in the right direction, or so I thought. I think you know where this is going, right? Every time you think you have OCD beat, it's simply waiting for you in the shadows.

In this case, it was waiting for me in Russia.

That year, Hockey Canada and the Russian Ice Hockey Federation put on an eight-game series that would emulate the 1972 Summit Series between the Soviet Union and Canada, except this series would be played with juniors aged 16 to 19. There would be four games played in Russia and then four in Canada. I'd be coaching alongside Brent Sutter, Peter DeBoer, Benoit Groulx and Craig Hartsburg.

The team flew to Moscow and trained there before heading to different cities scattered around Russia for the four games there. The first night we were there, Hockey Canada took the entire training staff and coaches for dinner. After an amazing meal, we took a taxi to a nightclub in Moscow. I'd had a few drinks, was tired from the long flight over and wanted to leave the club and walk back to the hotel. Brad Pascall and Craig

187

Hartsburg were feeling the same, and we headed back together. It was around midnight and pitch dark. I had to stop to pee, and we were only halfway home, so I stepped into a random alleyway off the main street to relieve myself.

I had just finished doing up my zipper when, out of nowhere, an unmarked white Volkswagen van screeched to a halt in front of us. Four large henchman-type guys got out of the van, grabbed me and threw me into the back of the van. They all had police hats on, but I got the strong suspicion that they weren't really police. A man in the back leaned forward out of the shadows, and all I could understand was him repeating, "Passport! Passport! Passport!" Thankfully, from playing with other Russian players over the years, I knew that in Russia, money talks. I opened my wallet and pulled out a couple American $100 bills and handed them to him. He snatched the money from my hand. The van was still stopped. He motioned to one of the men and they grabbed me and tossed me out onto the pavement. They all jumped back in, closed the doors and sped off into the night. I was lying on the ground, shaken but unhurt. Brad and Craig were in complete shock and couldn't speak. They both looked at me, and finally Brad said, "Hirschey, I thought you were dead." He wasn't kidding.

It was the best $200 I ever spent . . . and it was on a piss.

I should've known it was a sign of things to come on that trip. I shook off the previous night's debacle, and a couple nights later, we ended up heading to some other club after dinner. As I was walking in the door, I scratched my arm on a scaffolding pole. I didn't think anything about it at the time and went inside. As we were leaving, one of the team doctors we took on overseas trips looked at my arm. He said, "Holy shit, Hirschey! How did that happen?"

I looked down and I had a scratch from my elbow to my wrist. It wasn't deep but it looked worse than it was. I told the doctor what happened, and he just offhandedly said, "Hirschey, you have to be careful where you cut yourself in Russia."

And that was it. The trigger. My OCD immediately flared up. It was like an alarm went off inside my skull. The voice was screaming at me. While the doctor was talking about things such as a possible infection, my OCD was convincing me that he was talking about contracting HIV. My OCD was saying,

What if you didn't cut it on the scaffolding, but cut it inside the club? What if it was on a dirty needle that was sticking out of the couch we were sitting on? What if you rubbed your arm on it? Do you know for sure it was the scaffolding? What if it was from an IV drug user in the club? Whatifwhatifwhatifwhatif?

Round and round we went, inside my brain. The fight was on. My irrational brain was making up horrific *what if?* scenarios, and my rational brain was trying to fight back. The waves of relentless anxiety had returned, and my head felt like it was going to explode. My irrational brain was screaming at me. *What if you have HIV? What if you give it to the players and the coaching staff? It will be a national scandal. It will be your fault and you will be shunned back home by people forever.*

The next two weeks were complete hell. I would ask our team doctor over and over, looking for reassurance that I didn't get HIV, and no matter how many times he told me no, it didn't matter. I wasn't on my medication, and there was no chance of getting any in Russia. I was back to daily panic attacks, just trying to survive, hoping that I wouldn't lose my job. I didn't want anyone to know I had a diagnosable mental health issue, even though I was a coach now. The taboo was still too strong in my mind. I was constantly late for team meetings, I was making excuses of not feeling well, and I could tell they were wondering what was going on with me.

We played our final game in Omsk, and the bus was scheduled to leave early the next morning to go to the airport in order to head back home. There were still four games left to play in Canada. I fell into a deep sleep and woke up to Scott Salmond banging on my door. The bus was to leave at 5:30 a.m. I looked at my clock. It was 5:32! *Oh shit*, I thought. I scrambled to get dressed, grabbed my bags and ran onto the bus. I was already 15 minutes late and the players, coaches and staff were waiting for me. As a coach, I needed to be a good role model. I sat down in my seat, embarrassed, ashamed and disappointed in myself. I had been so busy obsessing the night before that I forgot to set my alarm. I was exhausted from days of panic attacks. I hated my brain. I hated myself for being who I was. I looked out the window of the bus and tears streamed down my face.

We were halfway around the world, and the trip back to Canada felt like it took forever. I was exhausted from the trip, but mainly from fighting my own brain. When we got back to Canada, I kept getting asked if I was okay. People on the staff could clearly tell that something was wrong. I withdrew from everyone. I could barely keep my eyes open during games, and I wasn't eating team meals. I kept using the excuse that I couldn't get used to the time change from Russia.

Brent Sutter was the head coach, and I could tell he was concerned about me. We chartered from Saskatoon to Red Deer, and he called me up to the front of the plane to sit with him. I sat down beside him, and he asked me if I was okay. I said, "Yeah, I'm okay. You know, the time zone thing. Just tired."

He looked at me again, paused and asked me if there was more going on than that. I got nervous. I hadn't told anyone about my mental health issues, and I was still terrified for anyone in the hockey world to find out. I needed to think quick. I was in survival mode.

So I told him that my family was having issues with my brother and that I was worried about him harming himself. In reality, I was talking about myself. I needed help and I was having suicidal thoughts again. But I was terrified of this hockey legend looking at me like I was crazy. What I came to find out over the next hour on that flight was that Brent Sutter is the type of guy who would give anyone the shirt off his back. I had him labelled as a stoic cowboy who was tough as nails; I thought that in his mind, feelings and emotions were for the weak and were not discussed. Boy, was I wrong. I never came completely clean to him, but he talked to me about a lot of things that day. He was empathetic, genuine and completely non-judgmental. It was another one of those little moments that probably saved my life, and I'm sure to this day Brent has no idea what he did for me on that flight.

The last four games mercifully ended with a stop in Vancouver, and I hurried back home to Vegas. I went straight to my doctor. I needed to get back on my medication immediately. He ended up putting me on Paxil. It took about two weeks for the meds to kick in, but slowly, I started to function again. The medication took the edge off and was exactly what I needed. The thoughts slowed down and weren't screaming at me anymore. I still needed to get therapy, but I was feeling better and hated the drive to LA, so I decided screw it, I would just stay on the meds forever. The medication worked well for me, and I was so frustrated with the difficulty of finding a therapist in Vegas who could help me, so I again relied solely on medication with no therapy. That was a big mistake.

I got through one more season with Hockey Canada, winning another gold medal, but I was always worried about what everyone thought of me after the previous summer. I was embarrassed and ashamed of the things that had happened, which in my head means it's time to cut and run and go somewhere new. It was just like going from team to team, or house to house in the minors, or living situation to living situation when I was younger. I was always trying to run from my own brain.

The following season, because of the success I'd had on the ice with Team Canada, I found a new home as the Toronto Maple Leafs goaltending coach. The Leafs were in a complete rebuild. Cliff Fletcher was the acting GM at the time, and I was hired by him and Ron Wilson, the head coach. Brian Burke came in as president and general manager of the Leafs in November 2008 after I'd been hired. That was not good for me.

Brian knew me from Vancouver. He knew my history. He

knew all the strange things that had happened and were said about me. My reputation from hiding my mental illness would again come back to bite me in the ass. He was the guy who finally shipped me out of Vancouver when I was a player, so I didn't exactly feel safe when he got to Toronto. To be fair to Brian, I didn't exactly endear myself with him in Toronto, either. We were in the coach's office, sitting around with Burkie and the rest of the coaches, bullshitting about hockey and players, when I stepped right in it. There was a small child in the office who I hadn't met before, playing and bouncing around on the floor, staying close to Brian. I looked at Brian right in the eyes and asked, "Oh, is that your grandchild there?"

The room went completely silent. Burkie looked at me and said, "No, Hirschey. That's my *kid*."

Whoopsie.

From there, through my own ignorance, history would repeat itself again. As always, after a time of feeling great, I eventually got complacent with my OCD, and I went off my medication. Months had gone by since the scratch in Russia, and I never felt sick, so the thought of having HIV subsided to a whisper. I felt the stigma attached to medication in the hockey community and the world at large, and my goal was always to get off the pills, because in my mind, real men didn't need medication. I felt somewhere deep down, because of the hockey culture that I'd been steeped in, that I was less of a man for taking them. What a moron I was to think that.

Sure enough, I relapsed with my OCD once again. I was in the Leafs locker room one morning before practice, and I shook hands with one of the trainers to say hello. When he turned to walk away, I noticed he was slightly bleeding on the back of his neck from a pimple. I immediately remembered shaking his hand. I scoured my right hand for any cuts he could have bled on. I had a scabbed blister on my right hand from shooting pucks on goalies. My OCD went ballistic. My head was about to explode. I was in another one. Over a damn pimple.

I went through all the questions: *Did he have blood on his hands? What if he touched my blister?* Round and round it went. The panic attacks, the overwhelming anxiety. The *what if?* questions.

HIVHIVHIVHIVSICKSICKSICKWHATIFHEHASIT-WHATIFWHATIFHEDOESHEDOESHEDOESHEDOES

YOU DO YOU DO YOU

YOU'LL GIVE IT TO YOUR KIDS WHATIFWHATIF-

WHATIF

I was in survival mode again. I went back to the hotel after practice, and the next day I flew back to Las Vegas.

Thankfully my schedule was week on, week off in Toronto, so I was able to get home, but I was in rough shape. I told my wife I was struggling again. I couldn't do it anymore. I needed to find therapy, and in Las Vegas. I was becoming hopeless that I would ever get rid of my OCD or find someone who could help me. So I went on the internet. I thought I needed more Cognitive Behavioural Therapy because that's what everyone always told me. I just googled "CBT Las Vegas."

To my surprise, a clinic in Las Vegas popped up. It was called the CBT Center of Las Vegas. I called and made an appointment immediately. I walked in, sat down and told the psychiatrist everything. To my surprise, he had just moved to Vegas from New York and was a specialist in OCD. He told me all he did for years and years at Hofstra University was treat people with my condition. It was pure luck, nothing else.

We immediately got to work. He helped me by teaching me to separate my OCD from myself. We started on a new therapy called ERP—Exposure Response Prevention. In a nutshell, ERP is like CBT on steroids, and it was the hardest thing I have ever done, but it worked. It's like staring the dragon right in the face. My therapy was to prick my finger daily as many times as I could. It had to be hard enough that I was actively bleeding from a tiny pinprick while I went along with my day, doing my normal routine. It was a minuscule amount of blood to the average person, but it was enough for me to be severely triggered. I had to do things like actively bleeding while I hugged my kids, or I had to touch things around the house and walk away without cleaning up the blood. I had to do it in the car, too. Again, to the average person? This is maybe a little bit icky, or maybe it sounds like nothing at all.

For me, it was like nails on a chalkboard times 10 billion.

It was awful, point blank. The anxiety from it brought me to my knees again. I only stuck with it because I so desperately wanted to get better, and I had tried everything else. My anxiety got so bad again that when I went back to Toronto for work, I

THE SAVE OF MY LIFE

felt completely trapped. I couldn't stand being inside my own brain for another minute. I was just so tired from all the years of ups and downs and pain and hope and setbacks and love and anger and fear. I was right back on that cliff in Kamloops again, staring out into the abyss. I didn't want to go on.

I called my psychiatrist from the hotel that night and told him that I was worried I was going to kill myself.

He knew how to handle me. He calmly asked me how I was going to do it. I told him I didn't know, maybe I would use the electric cord from the iron in the room. Then he calmly talked me down from my hysteria, and then he said, "I'll tell you what. Let's get you back on your medication and go from there." I agreed. There was no big revelation. I didn't see a light come down from the heavens. I didn't get a message from God. I didn't realize some hidden trauma from childhood or anything. Honestly, I just went back on my meds and slowly started to climb out of that dark, endless, bottomless hole once more.

With mental health, people always want some kind of easy *answer*. They want you to tell them some kind of secret password. But there is no easy answer. There is no password. Hell, there is no book, even this one you are reading. This is just the experience of one guy. This is just a long, strange trip inside my brain.

Eventually, through a lot of hard work, I came around. I evened out. I no longer feared HIV. I didn't fear blood. I didn't worry about hurting my family. I don't have any magic words for this part. If there was a special breakthrough, it was that ERP therapy taught me that my OCD was like a third person in a conversation who wasn't invited, and who I didn't need to listen to. It taught me to accept my thoughts for what they were—just passing *thoughts*, not reality—and that there is no such thing as 100 percent certainty.

Do you know what my mantra became?

This is going to sound almost ridiculous, it's so simple.

Whenever my thoughts would become triggered by something and I worried that I was going to hurt my family or that I had HIV, I started telling myself, *Maybe I do. Maybe I don't. I don't care.*

Maybe I do. Maybe I don't. I don't care. Maybe I do. Maybe I don't. I don't care.

When that became my mantra, it flipped a switch for me. When people have undiagnosed OCD, they think they're crazy. They think they're monsters. They think they don't care about other people, because if they care about other people, then why are they always thinking that they're going to hurt them? But the nasty irony about OCD is that those who suffer from it actually care *too* much. They're over-sensitive to every possible danger, to every thought that they could possibly hurt someone else. They care in overdrive. They care to the point of pure obsession.

So when I started telling myself, *I don't care,* it felt strangely freeing. For most of my life, all I ever did, to the point of obsession, was care.

I will always have mental health issues. I work on them every day. But through therapy, meditation and hard work, I have gone on to live a great life and the OCD is now a whisper.

Unfortunately, by that point, it had done so much damage to my relationships that I still had to pay another price.

13

This is, in many ways, the hardest part of the book. I know that probably seems strange. "Hirschey, you almost drove your car off a cliff, you told your mom you wanted to jump off the Empire State Building in the middle of a Stanley Cup run, you tried to break your own hand with a stick blade in a Marriott, you had an out-of-body experience during a Canucks practice, you almost got *Taken* in Moscow, and then you broke down in tears in front of all the boys on the Team Canada bus. I mean, *what else?*"

The thing is, when it comes to mental health, the most difficult part isn't your own pain. The hardest part is how it affects your family. A lot of what I put my wife through over the years, I honestly do not even remember. My life was enveloped in a thick fog. I was *not there*. I was off in another dimension, dealing with the voices screaming at me in my brain 24/7. By 2011, a few years into my retirement, our marriage was starting to crumble. I had moved on from the Leafs and was coaching for the St. Louis Blues, and I was on the road all the time. It was a vestige of my old life, from when I was really sick. And it's a habit that I still have to this day. Somewhere deep down, I will always be running from my demons. I like to be on the move. Even now, when I talk on the phone, I like to walk around, or drive somewhere in my car. Something about movement soothes me. It was no different when I was coaching.

That 2011–12 season, I was living in St. Louis and my wife and kids were living in Arizona. It was the best thing for our marriage at the time. My kids didn't want to change schools yet again. It wasn't fair to them. So I would commute from

St. Louis whenever I could, and it's a good thing that I did, because one day that year when I was at home, my daughter took me aside and confided in me.

She told me straight out, "Dad, I'm going to be honest with you. I'm starting to have some scary thoughts in my head that I can't really understand."

She was only 13 years old at the time, and I'm so proud of her for having the courage to tell me what she was going through. As a father, hearing something like that is so terrifying. You never want to think of your children suffering. But for me, it really hit me in the gut, because I always worried that I would pass this burden down to my kids. I knew how bad it could get. The thought of my wonderful, kind daughter having to live through the hell that I did was a fate worse than death.

We immediately got her professional help. The therapist quickly diagnosed her with OCD, but thankfully, because of our early intervention, she never got to that dangerous place that I did with my own OCD. In our home, because of what happened to me, I always talked about mental health with my children. I educated them on it and made it safe for them to tell me anything. I had learned through my treatment that mental health issues can be partially genetic, and it's so important for a parent to know what to look for. I always told my kids that if they ever felt that something in their brains wasn't right or they were having thoughts they were concerned about, that they were to tell me right away—that they could talk to me about *anything*, especially anything going on in their heads. I drilled that into them from the time they were three or four years old.

That might sound extreme, but mental health problems can start as early as four, and the most common time for a mental health problem to surface is between the ages of 12 and 24. This is why our school systems, teachers and parents need to play such a key role in prevention and early diagnosis. Our kids need to understand that mental health is *health*, and it's okay to not be okay. We need to give them the information they need, especially during that vulnerable and confusing time when you're in middle school and high school. My daughter is a prime example of how open dialogue in the home and early education make mental health issues much easier to treat successfully. She will never get to the point that I did.

After that season of commuting back and forth for my job, I still had two years on my contract with St. Louis. My wife and I had been through a lot together over the years, and the moving, along with the lifestyle, had taken its toll. The stress of going from team to team during my playing career, and of my mental health issues, was difficult to recover from.

I believe everyone should have a therapist on hand like we do a doctor, and I went to see my therapist on more than one occasion to discuss what to do about my marriage. This was not OCD therapy. This was real life. I took it very seriously. I didn't want a divorce, but I could see it headed in that direction. A good therapist won't tell you what to do with a major life decision like getting a divorce, but they can help you come to your own answer.

I spent most of that next season in St. Louis, and I was leaning towards divorce. My heart broke for my children most of all, but the situation just seemed too toxic for everyone involved. When I came home from St. Louis at the end of the 2012–13 season, I finally asked my wife for a divorce.

I can't and won't speak for her role in our divorce. That's

her story to tell. In every divorce, it takes two to tango, and I can only speak for me and what I felt went wrong. What really matters is that we raised three beautiful, healthy children, and I was thankful for that.

Divorce sucks. It hurts, it's painful, and in the end, nobody wins. I didn't regret my decision to end my marriage, but it had been a long road, and breaking up my family was the hardest decision I had ever made. When I got my divorce decree, legally ending my marriage, I felt no joy. All I felt was failure. The heartbreak and feeling of failure sucks. It's pain I never wanted to feel again.

I learned some hard lessons. I thought that getting back into the NHL was my obligation to my family, and that was how I could best support them. As an athlete, I focused more on how to improve my game than on what was most important, and that was my family. I went on to the next team more than once without looking back, and I left my wife to pick up the pieces back home. That's on me and is mine to own. But I think it explains why so many athletes end up getting divorced, even if they aren't suffering from mental health issues.

In a professional athlete's marriage, it's very easy for a spouse to lose themselves, and their entire identity, and what they bring to the table in the relationship. It becomes more about our on-ice performance. If I played well, I might get another contract; if I didn't play well, the family was looking for a new job and moving again. Players get traded, sent down or moved to another city all the time, and spouses are left at home to figure everything out. They have to leave their friends and go to a new place where they are starting at the beginning again where they don't know anyone. Add in finding new doctors and schools for the kids—it's a lot for anyone. It's also very possible that the next season after that, and the next season after that, you may be doing it all over again. It takes a lot of understanding and a special person to be an athlete's spouse.

A spouse's identity can easily become their husband's identity. My wife could be walking down the street and a person would point and say, "Hey, that's Corey Hirsch's wife," or she would get introduced to other people at dinner as "This is Corey Hirsch's wife." It's not a great existence living in someone else's shadow, and it can definitely cause resentment and loss of self-esteem, among other things. For us, there was just too much damage to repair.

That 2013–14 season was also my last with St. Louis. I was going through the divorce, and I could sense that the organization thought it was affecting me personally. They supported me, but I knew my days were numbered. I wasn't as demanding as I should have been with Jaroslav Halak, and even though he had played well for us, there were issues we needed to move on from. When our general manager, Doug Armstrong, heard that All-Star Buffalo Sabres goaltender Ryan Miller was available, he asked my opinion and I gave the thumbs-up that Ryan would be an upgrade from our current goaltending situation. After all, Miller was the goalie who almost beat the powerhouse Canadian team in the Olympic final in Vancouver in 2010.

The NHL entered a two-week break to participate in the Sochi Olympics during the 2013–14 NHL season. Doug went over as a consultant with Hockey Canada, and when he came back, he pulled the trigger on a monster deal that sent Halak, Chris Stewart, a prospect and two draft picks to the Buffalo Sabres for Ryan Miller and Steve Ott.

Miller had starred with Buffalo for nine seasons and had never been traded before. His wife was an actress living in Los Angeles, and he seemed to never get his footing in St. Louis. He was acquired with the intent that he'd be the final piece the Blues needed to contend for the Stanley Cup. Doug went all in.

Miller had played really well for us during the final games of the regular season, but in a seven-game series, there were some things in his game that I saw that were being exposed, and he struggled in the playoffs. There were only weeks left in the season, so helping maintain Miller's game was the only thing I was able to do as a coach. There was no time for tweaks or suggestions for improvement on things I thought he could be better at. A goaltending coach would never change a goaltender's style of play during the playoffs. It would be similar to Tiger Woods's golf coach trying to change his swing in the middle of the PGA Masters Tournament at Augusta. It would be a disaster.

In the opening round against the Blackhawks, our biggest rivals, we won the first two games in overtime, but then Chicago won four straight games and we were eliminated. Doug was absolutely furious; so furious that he was too angry to meet with us at the end of the season. He told the coaching staff to go home and wait, as there would be some changes.

Three weeks later I got a phone call and was told by Doug that he was making a change in my department. I knew I took the bullet for the Ryan Miller deal. When a team owner looks at the GM at the end of the season after an early exit and asks what went wrong, they definitely aren't going to blame themselves. Coaches are easy to pick off, and assistant coach Gary Agnew and I took the bullets that year.

I applied for three jobs that summer: Buffalo, Carolina and Calgary. I went to the NHL Draft in Philadelphia and interviewed first with Ted Nolan of the Sabres. We had a great chat. I was impressed with Ted, as he was an open and honest guy. I was hoping to work with him, but he hired Arturs Irbe and I didn't get the job.

Carolina wasn't going to interview me. They had heard all the things about me that circulated over the years and said they weren't interested. At the draft, I talked to their coach, Bill Peters, who I knew from a stint with Hockey Canada, and

Carolina finally agreed to an interview. The interview went well, but again, they hired someone else.

The last team left that had an opening was Calgary. I interviewed with GM Brad Treliving, but again, I finished second and was still looking for a job.

So now what?

I was getting divorced, and with no other NHL goaltending coaching opportunities available, I was really getting nervous about my future. I woke up every day for two months drenched in anxiety and depression. What the hell was I going to do? I had three kids to take care of!

The NHL season started, and out of sheer boredom, I sat on my couch and tweeted. Sometimes it was funny, but mostly it was just opinionated things about NHL games. In mid-October, I tweeted about some game, and I wasn't even sure what I'd said. I went to bed thinking nothing of it. I woke up the next morning and my phone was ringing. It was Elliotte Friedman from Sportsnet and *Hockey Night in Canada*. I answered my phone wondering what the hell Elliotte Friedman would want with me.

Elliotte told me that he and some producers had been watching my Twitter account and liked what I was saying about the games. He asked me if I could bring that personality to television. For a second, I thought I was being pranked. Then I said, "You're damn right I can" and jumped at the chance. Two months later, I was on TV doing panels on NHL games for Sportsnet. Executive producer Mitch Kerzner even put me on *Hockey Night in Canada.* Being in the media and on TV was always my post-career dream, and it started with a tweet. However, like I was told by my equipment rep years earlier, I had to put myself out there if I wanted to be noticed. In a roundabout way, through tweets, I did just that.

I commuted out of Phoenix for the next two seasons, and it was a blast. I loved doing television. Unfortunately, Sportsnet had paid a lot of money for the rights to the broadcast NHL games and decided they needed to cut the budget. My contract, along with the contracts of many others at Sportsnet who travelled, was not renewed the following season, and I found myself unemployed.

Again.

Here I was back in the same place, wondering what I was going to do with my life. I thought about making a complete career change and getting out of hockey altogether, but hockey was all I knew. As luck and timing would have it, my life would yet again take another turn that following season, when, out of work, I went to an Arizona Coyotes game in Glendale.

A friend of mine, an NHL agent, was at the game. I ran into him, and he was sitting with a hockey player I recognized but who I realized was not from either of the teams playing on the ice. We were sitting in the stands. Something wasn't right, as this player was an active player. He should have been with his team.

I asked him what he was doing there. "I'm in rehab," he replied.

I said, "Oh, what did you injure?" I was thinking it was a physical rehab.

He said slowly, "No, I'm in rehab," and that's when the light bulb went on that he was in an outpatient clinic for substance abuse. I knew he was probably lonely, not being from there, so I asked him to go for coffee. He agreed, and the next day I picked him up and we went to Starbucks.

Since he was in rehab, I knew there was most likely a mental health issue, so we sat down and I spilled out my story to him. I had never told another player my story. In fact, I hadn't really told it to anyone other than those close to me.

After I was finished, he looked at me and said, "Oh my God! That's exactly what happened to me!"

I was taken aback. He told me his own mother had been forced to resuscitate him from an overdose. He admitted that he should have been dead.

I had never met anyone with a story like mine, and it was the first time I realized how deadly untreated OCD can be and that there were others out there suffering like I did. That's when I decided that other people needed to hear my story. I realized that it just might save someone from taking their life.

One problem . . . I had no idea how to make it happen.

I was terrified about putting my life out there, but I knew I wanted to, so I called some of my friends who had already come forward with their own personal stories. My first call was to Clint Malarchuk, a fellow goalie and friend of mine. His book, *The Crazy Game*, is one of the most incredible things a person can ever read about a man that struggled during his NHL career with mental health and alcohol abuse. He told me that speaking out was the best thing he ever did in his life, and not to be afraid.

A few weeks later, I met with Michael Landsberg, a broadcaster and mental health advocate, at a coffee shop in Toronto, and he told me the exact same thing: "It will be the best thing you ever do in your life."

Things after that started to come together in an almost bizarre fashion.

Sadly, and unexpectedly, just before Christmas of 2016, the coach who had given me my first NHL start, Ron Smith, passed away. I knew his son Devin and asked if I could speak at the funeral. Ron had done so much for me, and I felt I needed to pay my respects to him. I flew from Arizona to Toronto and spoke at the funeral. After the service was over, I went back to the family's house and sat in the living room with all the others who had come back. I sat beside a wonderful woman named Lana, who I'd spoken to briefly at the celebration of life service. Lana lived in Victoria, British Columbia, and asked me what I was doing for work these days.

I don't know why, but I opened up to Lana and told her my whole story. I didn't even know her. I told Lana I wasn't sure how to get my story out there and that I was thinking of writing a book. Lana lit up and told me that she and her business partner, Catherine, oversaw the foundations for Trevor Linden as well as the Sedins in Vancouver, and that she and Catherine would help me. That conversation changed the course of my life.

Devin Smith, who worked with the NHLPA, kindly gave me tickets to all the events at the NHL All-Star Game in LA. It was his way of thanking me for speaking at his dad's celebration of life. So I met Lana in LA, and unbeknownst to me, she had already contacted a wonderful woman who was working with the NHL named Jessica Berman. Jessica helped set me up with a man named Frank Buonomo of the *Players' Tribune*, an online sports publication started in 2014 by New York Yankees baseball legend Derek Jeter. The wheels were in motion. I went back to Arizona and interviewed with writer Sean Conboy, the executive editor, and we got to work on my story. He wrote the guts of it and sent the story back to me to edit for accuracy. I got a chill reading it, as he absolutely nailed it. It was scary how accurate and powerful the piece was.

The article, titled "Dark, Dark, Dark, Dark, Dark, Dark, Dark, Dark," launched on the *Players' Tribune* on February 16, 2017. I was absolutely terrified to be so transparent and put my life out there for the world to read and judge, yet within two hours of going online, the article went viral. The response was instantaneous and overwhelming. It had almost a million hits in under two hours. I was getting calls and messages from family, friends and people all over the continent. The love, support and sincere thank-yous from people were something I never expected, and it was overwhelming. People were praising my story. The raw candour and transparency had blown the doors off of the mental health conversation.

Truth be told, I was mostly nervous about what my peers would think. The article was somewhat of an apology to the guys I played with who saw my meltdown in the dressing room in New Jersey back in 1997. It was my way of letting them know what I was going through at the time.

Clint Malarchuk and Michael Landsberg were right. Telling the truth was the most freeing thing I've ever done. Going into the depths of my darkness let the light in.

14

Approximately six days prior to the original *Players' Tribune* article coming out in 2017, I met a beautiful woman online, who will remain nameless to protect her identity. She lived close to me in Scottsdale, Arizona. She had just gotten out of a relationship and was dipping her toe back in the water. I, however, was ready to fall in love. She was originally from Edmonton and grew up an Oilers fan. I was from Calgary and grew up a Flames fan. If you know anything about the Flames-Oilers rivalry and the Battle of Alberta, you know that she and I had a lot to talk about.

We had our first date at an Arizona Coyotes game against the Pittsburgh Penguins on February 11, 2017. I met her at the bar inside the Keg restaurant in Phoenix prior to the game. I was sitting alone at the bar, and in she walked like a hurricane. I will never forget how much energy she brought into the room. She sat down beside me, and I was immediately consumed by her charm, beauty and humorous nature.

The hockey game was great. We talked and laughed through the entire game. It was so good, I didn't even know who won, and I didn't want the date to end. We went out for drinks back in Scottsdale after the game and ran into a friend of mine, Jamie Ram, who was sitting with Rick Tocchet, an assistant coach with the Penguins. Rick owned a place in Scottsdale, and the team was staying overnight. I had met him on a few occasions before but didn't know him very well. My date had never met him. We sat down with Jamie and Rick and were making small talk when Rick asked her how we had met.

Without missing a beat, she said, "Farmers Only dot com."

I looked at her, shocked that she had said that. Rick was being polite and didn't flinch but was looking at me like, "Really,

Hirschey?" I started laughing, then she broke into a laugh, and it was apparent that this girl would not be like anyone I had met before. It was the first time we'd met and hung out together, but I felt like I had known her my entire life.

We went on nine more dates. I know because I counted them. I'd had my heart broken once before and wasn't about to let that happen again. It was a late Friday night, and we were sitting in her backyard when I asked her where she thought our relationship was going, to which she replied, "I'm sorry, but I will never date you."

I was shocked and pissed that she was thinking we'd just be friends. I had put in a lot of time with her and really liked her. I got up from my seat, looked at her calmly and said, "I'm not here to be your friend." I then walked out the door. She was stunned. I don't think she had ever had anyone walk out on her like that. I wanted to date her. I didn't want her as a friend, and I made it clear.

Two days went by without any contact between us, and I figured it was officially done. *Back to the drawing board*, I thought. I was sitting at home alone on a Monday afternoon when I got a cute video message from her.

"Why are you sending me this?" I asked.

She messaged back, "Because I miss you."

We were inseparable from that moment on.

This woman was athletic as well as beautiful. She could play hockey, ski, golf and could cook an amazing turkey dinner for 10 while looking stunning doing it. Sometimes we would play hockey at midnight in her backyard after getting back from a night out. I would get in net and she would take shots on me. Sometimes she would get in net and we'd laugh our asses off as I took shots on her. I was falling hard for her. It was perfect. Too perfect.

On the outside, she portrayed a beautiful, fun, funny, shining light. On the inside, what she didn't let many see, was a beaten-down little girl in every category imaginable: emotionally, physically, spiritually and financially. She was broken in a million pieces, and any love I had for her could never be enough to put her back together.

When she opened up to me, she talked a lot about being abandoned in previous relationships. When she wasn't working,

THE SAVE OF MY LIFE

she would spend two to three days a week lying in bed from severe fatigue. She had been diagnosed with chronic Epstein-Barr Syndrome, the medical term for chronic mononucleosis, and although she owned a design company, having to sleep for 48 hours straight at times put a huge strain on her ability to keep up and make money.

We were looking at photos one night when she showed me a picture of a massive red mark on her arm from a bug bite that she had to have antibiotics to treat. I told her I thought she was misdiagnosed and should get tested for Lyme disease, but she never did.

She told me she had been diagnosed with PTSD and was on prescription medication, but that wasn't enough to slow the past from haunting her. I saw her suffer from panic attacks, but I had no idea how bad the situation really was. She hid her problems deep inside so that she wouldn't be a burden on anyone. She mostly hid it with a pretty face and a gorgeous smile. I loved her, but my love couldn't change her past. I met her too late for that.

We had been dating a few months when Sportsnet picked up the rights for the radio broadcasts of Vancouver Canucks games. Out of work, I needed the job, so I interviewed and was hired to do colour commentary for all Canucks games. It meant I would have to move to Vancouver. She shared custody of her two boys and would be limited to being able to visit me when she didn't have them. She needed me more than I knew, and when I left for Vancouver, everything took a turn as things began to unravel for her.

I never knew the extent of she was going through inside—she didn't talk much about her mental health. We were lying in bed together and talking about gratitude. She was not very religious, but I asked her to pray with me to the universe or whatever she believed in for something to come to her that she wanted in her life.

She looked at me, paused and said, "I pray every night."

I was a bit taken aback. I hadn't known her to believe in praying for anything. I asked her, "What do you pray for?"

To which she softly replied, "To make it through one more day."

She didn't want more money, or a shiny new car, she just wanted God, the universe or whatever a person believes in to give her the strength to get through one more day. Not a week. Not a month or a year. Just one more day.

She came out to Vancouver to visit me a few times early in the season. With a lack of work projects, she was struggling to pay the bills, and I helped her as much as I could. We spent Christmas night of 2017 together at her home. She cooked an incredible turkey dinner for me and all of our kids, but something that night about her was off. For the first time, I started to worry about her, but I just didn't know how seriously things were unravelling. When I went back to Vancouver after Christmas for work, she was spending most of her days in bed, crushed by Epstein-Barr, sleeping three or four days a week.

I asked a couple of her friends to keep an eye on her, but sometimes that was what she did—she slept for days on end, and there wasn't much anyone could do about it. When I returned to Arizona for the All-Star break in mid-January, she started to push me away hard. This was not the girl I knew anymore. She was really angry, upset and accusing me of things that weren't happening. She withdrew from her friends. She was upset at the world and was filled with negativity. I kept telling her how much

I cared for her and loved her, but it was as though there was a force field around her brain and nothing positive was getting in. No matter how much I told her I loved her and how great she was, it didn't matter—I just couldn't get through to her.

On January 19, she broke up with me. I was devastated. I tried desperately to get her back. The following week, I flew back to Arizona and begged her to have dinner with me. She agreed, but dinner was a disaster. She tore a strip off me, and she left before finishing dinner. I was distraught. I didn't know who this woman was anymore. It wasn't the person I had known and loved. I went home crushed.

I couldn't sleep. At two a.m., I texted her and told her that I loved her but wouldn't contact her again. My phone rang almost immediately. It was her, and her tone was 180 degrees different. I was talking to the girl I knew again. I didn't care how or why, but it was her, and we talked until the sun came up. I went over to her house. It was a Sunday, and we spent an amazing day together. She came over to me in the middle of the day and hugged me hard. Then she stopped, pushed me away and looked at me. "I can't understand why I'm so happy right now."

It was a strange thing to say, and I didn't understand what she meant. It was as though the light that was her was flickering in and out of working properly.

I had to fly back to Vancouver the next day. As I was leaving, she came to the front door with me. I hugged her and told her that I loved her. She told me that she loved me back, and as I drove away, I looked in the rear-view mirror. She was standing in the doorway for a moment and paused, almost as if she *knew*. She then slowly closed the door behind her.

I felt empty driving away, as though I would never be back there.

I got back to Vancouver, and two days later, things went south again. I was confused. I tried to tell her how amazing I thought she was and how much I loved her, but again, nothing was getting through. Saturday morning of that weekend, I was very upset and told her I couldn't take it anymore, that she needed to get some help.

Twenty-four hours later, on February 4, 2018, I woke up and headed to the airport to get on the plane. I was with the Canucks, travelling to Florida for an eastern swing. It was

Super Bowl Sunday. After a six-hour plane ride, we landed in Fort Lauderdale. I checked my phone, hoping to hear from her, but there was nothing. We bused to the hotel located directly across from the beach. The sun was setting and it was a beautiful Florida evening. I went for a long walk on the beach that night around midnight after watching the Super Bowl with the guys and having a few beers. The waves were crashing up on my feet, and I remember feeling a sense of calm. I can't describe it, but it was a peaceful, calm feeling like I was going to be okay. I walked barefoot in the sand with the bottom of my pants wet. The sound of the ocean was both beautiful and serene.

I went to bed late that night and fell into a deep sleep. I wanted to get back together with her. In my mind, I would give her some space, be patient, and she'd come around. I woke up at seven a.m. on February 5, and while eating breakfast, was thinking that it was a glorious day. I walked to the mall and bought a pair of sunglasses.

The day went by and it was quiet. She used to post a lot on social media, but on this day, there were no posts. I thought nothing of it. I went for dinner and I was at a table in a restaurant with some of the other broadcasters and Canucks staff when I got a note on Facebook Messenger from her father that I was to call him. The message said something strange had happened.

It didn't make sense. I had never before been messaged by her dad. I stepped outside and called him.

He told me he had some strange news.

"What is it?" I asked.

He was having trouble getting the words out, and I asked again. "What's wrong? What's going on?"

He told me that she had hurt herself.

"What do you mean, 'hurt herself'? Is she in the hospital? Is she okay? What happened?"

That's when he said the words that I never want to hear again; words a person should never have to hear.

He told me that she had taken her life.

I dropped to my knees right there in the parking lot, sobbing uncontrollably, pleading with him to tell me that it wasn't true, that there had been some sort of mistake.

I stood up and walked in circles, aimlessly, sobbing, trying to catch my breath. In complete shock, just saying, "No! No!

No! No! No! No!" over and over again, begging for it to not be true. Canucks TV play-by-play announcer John Shorthouse and two members of the Canucks staff, Mike Brown and Ben Brown, walked up and saw me. I dropped to my knees again in front of them and told them that my girlfriend was dead. They helped me up and took me to my room, where I called some of her friends and my mom. No one could believe it. There was nothing they could say or do to make it better.

The woman I loved was gone.

The next day, I took the first flight back to Arizona. I was so distraught that Dan Murphy, the Canucks in-game TV host, flew with me to help get me there. I couldn't stop crying, and there was nothing he could say or do to make it better.

I spent the next seven days in Arizona trying to put together the puzzle of her death. She was a 43-year-old mother of two. It just didn't make sense. She loved her boys more than anything. I was there. I saw it. I had to learn as much as I could about her death. I needed answers. And with suicide, you are often left with none.

Death by suicide is excruciatingly painful for those left

behind. She took all the answers with her. I would rather she had been killed in a car accident because at least then I could explain it. The question why will never get answered, and all the people she left behind, in some form or another, blame themselves.

I was destroyed inside. It put a hole in my soul that will never go away.

Putting what I knew together, the night she took her life she had been at a Super Bowl party at her friend Maria's house. She looked happy, taking pictures and having a good time. When she left, she told Maria she loved her. She seemed to be okay.

She didn't leave a note.

She was cremated with no service other than a small get-together with some close friends, arranged by Maria. Her ashes were flown back to Alberta. It happened so quickly, like she had never existed.

I blamed myself. How could I have not seen this coming? We shared so much! I told her all my struggles. I am a mental health advocate and yet I had no idea. She didn't tell me. She never told me the depth of what was going on, on the inside. I knew she was having a difficult time, but never in a million years did I think that she would take her life.

I barely functioned after that. I had never experienced depression on that level before. I had dealt with OCD, but this was different. I was suffering from severe depression. I fought to get out of bed daily and had a complete loss of joy in anything I did. I started my day in tears at the bottom of my shower, and it proceeded from there to sitting on a bar stool, drinking away any feelings that I had. I was looking for anything to take away the colossal level of pain I felt. There was no cure for grief, no magic pill, no amount of therapy that sped up the process, and I tried to drink my way around it.

Without a proper service for her, her best friend and I put together a small gathering in her hometown, where her ashes had already been buried with her grandparents. We said our final goodbyes to her on the weekend of her 44th birthday—July 14, 2018.

It gave me a small sense of closure, but I still hadn't fully dealt with the magnitude of her death. For the first 10 months after the suicide, I drank. A *lot*. Every day. I went through years of

OCD, and never once did I feel that I had a drinking problem. In fact, I stayed away from it. Depression was a different animal than anything I had experienced, and alcohol was that quick fix that helped me to forget. Substance abuse and mental health go hand in hand. This was a slippery slope I was getting myself onto. I was still working and functioning, but barely.

Things weren't getting any better months after she broke it off with me. In late December 2018, my parents celebrated their 50th wedding anniversary. My mom had bought a bottle of bourbon for guests, and I was a bourbon drinker. I started drinking that afternoon, one after another, and then finally passed out on my bed later that night. Thank God I didn't do anything stupid to embarrass myself. The next morning, Mom asked me, "That entire bottle of bourbon is gone. Did you drink it all?" I said, "No, there were others drinking it, too." I completely lied to my own mother. I knew that I had drunk the entire bottle.

Two scary things happen when you are drinking a lot. The first is you have to drink a lot more to get the same feeling again, and secondly, you don't get hungover anymore.

Two weeks after my parents' anniversary, I was in down-town Toronto. I found myself walking the streets at three in the morning, staggering and by myself. I was so hammered I didn't care if I lived or died. The next morning, I woke up starfished on my bed, still in my clothes from the night before, not know-ing how I got there. I gave my head a shake. I had three kids who needed me to be alive and be a dad. Anything could have happened to me!

I needed help. I was scared of losing everything—my family, my friends and my career. There were times on road trips where everybody would go back to their hotel rooms at night after dinner. I'd go to my room, too, but I'd wait until everyone was in their room, and I'd go back out again until two or three in the morning. By myself. There were many nights, too many to count, where I'd be sitting alone at one a.m. on a bar stool with tears streaming down my face.

I considered going into rehab or calling the NHL Alumni to see if there was an alcohol program available. Instead, I decided to call a friend of mine who I'd known for years. She was in recovery and was five years sober. I admitted to her that

I needed help. Without my realizing it, she put together an intervention with her, her sponsor and my former junior teammate Darryl Sydor. Darryl had struggled with alcohol, and he brought in Dr. Brian Shaw, a Toronto-based doctor who works for the NHLPA and co-founded the SABH (Substance Abuse and Behavioral Health) Program. I didn't realize while it was happening, but I was having an intervention!

Dr. Shaw suggested I check into a facility, but I didn't want to take the time out from my job, so I convinced them that I would try it on my own. Right then and there, scared to death of losing everything, I stopped drinking for almost two full months, started to eat right and exercise, and most importantly, I went back into therapy. Mostly, though, what I did was face my grief directly. I learned the hard way that the only path to healing is to feel the pain and go straight into it head on. Everybody wants to put a timeline on grief, but it's different for everyone, and only the person going through it knows when they are or aren't ready.

When I didn't have alcohol to anaesthetize my feelings and I had to deal with my issues, I had to let myself feel emotions again. I had to look at myself in the mirror and heal. What I tried to do with alcohol was sidestep the grieving process. You can't avoid grief. You can try, as I did, but the sadness won't go away until you feel it and deal with it. An incredible thing happened when I did that. My heart started to heal, my system reset, and I started to crawl out of the hole I was in.

I was very lucky to be part of a great organization like the NHL Alumni. I hadn't played a game in the NHL in over 15 years, and the NHL Alumni and Dr. Shaw were there for me when I needed them. The NHL and the NHL Alumni help many players who are struggling and convince them to go into therapy and/or rehab. They've saved more lives and have helped more players than the public will ever know about.

As part of my healing, I went to see a psychiatrist who specializes in dealing with the grief of suicides. He told me that my girlfriend's problems didn't just arise in the time we were together; they would have started in her childhood. She needed help as a teen. With no education in the schools and nowhere to turn, she would have gone untreated and undiagnosed into her adult years. With the onset of Epstein-Barr Syndrome, her health took a massive hit and she struggled to make money. Not able to afford medical treatment, she was failed again. She applied to get a home equity loan for financial help but was denied because she didn't have the credit or enough income. Failed by the system one last time.

I obviously disagreed with her taking her life, but I began to understand it. She was sick, not weak, and the system had failed her in so many ways.

Sadly, it's not an uncommon story.

I continued to look for answers. I went through old videos and screenshots that she took of her phone. Sadly, I found more failure. I stumbled onto finding out that she called her therapist as well as the suicide hotline a few months prior to her death. Again, no one, including the hotline, told me. If I'd known, I possibly could have helped her! I'm a big believer in suicide hotlines, and I understand confidentiality. But this isn't something a person should go through alone because it can be catastrophic. I didn't know she had made a previous attempt, and I didn't know that she called a suicide hotline. I couldn't see her mental health struggles. No one could. But if

I'd known, maybe I could have gotten her the proper help she needed.

The signs were there. Her feelings of being abandoned and alone, along with the anger and hopelessness. She had tried to take her life on more than one previous occasion prior to her death. That was a major sign she might try again! I was the closest person to her, and I needed to know the history. Secrets are toxic, and this secret kept me from knowing. If I suspect a person is suicidal, I tell someone. I tell the people who care and can watch for signs that they may attempt it again.

Mental health takes a village. It takes all of us.

I'm sure some saw her suicide as a selfish act. This would be the furthest thing from the truth. I saw first-hand how sick she was, the panic attacks, how she was failed by a broken system. She didn't want to die. She was exhausted, her brain was broken. She loved her boys more than anything, but it's very possible her brain was lying to her, telling her she was a burden, and that the world would be a better place without her. In her mind, there was no other way out. Completely depleted in all categories, finding dead ends at every turn, she had nothing left to give.

This woman had suffered with mental health for a long, long time, possibly since she was a kid. I'd been there, I'd had those same thoughts. My brain lied to me, too.

Sometimes I think that the only reason I am still here, telling my story, is through sheer luck. How many people in the hockey community didn't get those little breaks? How many people didn't have a Mike Burnstein or a Kennedy or a Dave Babych or a Brent Sutter to lean on at just the right moment?

How many lives could we have saved if someone had just said, "Hey buddy, how ya doin'? Are you okay? Do you need somebody to talk to?"

How many aren't here with us anymore?

How many can we still save?

15

One more day."

I quote her from the night I asked her to pray to a higher power or whatever she believed in for what she wanted. She had the simplest of requests: to make it through one more day. She didn't want a bigger car, or a nicer house. She wanted a day of good health. A day without panic attacks, a day without crippling anxiety, a day of peace without having to live in fear from her PTSD.

Tragically, in the early hours of February 5, 2018, she ran out of days.

I promised myself that I wouldn't let that happen ever again to anyone. I don't want another family or friend to have to feel what I felt; to go through what I did. And it wasn't just me. She left behind a lot of people who loved her, who will always be hurting.

If a person is ever finding it hard to go on, I want them to think only about making it through "one more day." Not tomorrow, not next week, or next month, but today. The best a person can do on any given day might be getting out of bed, and if that's all they can do then so be it, they should applaud themselves for it. Society pounds into us that having a high-powered career, making lots of money and having the perfect family defines success. Bullshit! Success is the best you can do at any given moment, and that may be as much as getting up, getting out of bed and getting dressed. There are days for me that getting up and having a shower is as great a victory as any win I ever had in the NHL. My friend Michael Landsberg, who struggles with depression and is the founder of Sick Not Weak, has a saying: "Be proud of the shower." I couldn't say it better myself.

Life does go on, and life does get better. Where someone's

life is in any given moment will not be where they will be a year later. Life changes through time, and time truly does heal, but I understand how people lose hope, as hope is tough to have when in the thick of it. I too struggled to see a future at the worst of times.

After her death, I was thinking of suicide daily, drinking heavily, and I fell into a deep depression, a depression to the depths that I had never experienced before. I found no joy in anything I had or did. I knew enough about mental health that my best chance at survival was to put together a support group. So I put together a list in my head of the people I could count on to call or text when things got really bad. One of those people was a female friend, and the other was a former teammate of mine. None of us lived in the same city, but that didn't matter. We have the technology, and a support group can be anywhere.

Her death brought a lot of "survivor guilt" for me and for those she left behind. It led me to suicidal thoughts. For someone like me, who had struggled with suicidal ideation and mental health, my brain would tell me the only way to see her again would be to join her. Deep down, I knew that was not the answer, but there were a lot of tough nights, nights in which I would text or call my female friend at one a.m., bawling my face off, telling her I couldn't do it anymore. I know it was tough on her, but she did all the right things. She listened, let me vent, and not once did she ever judge me. She did all the things a good friend listening to another friend in crisis would do. She encouraged me to get therapy and the help I needed, which I did. When I talk of those who are and those who aren't "your people," she is an example of someone who is. It wasn't every day, but after four or five of those difficult moments, we put together the simplest of plans to help me snap out of it when I would get like that. She was to remind me that when I got like that, I was to simply go to bed and go to sleep; that tomorrow would be a new day and that I just needed to get to it.

It was, in fact, a "One More Day" plan.

That simple plan worked because it kept me in check. It reminded me of the need to get to one more day. Not to worry about a week later, or a month, or a year, but to just get to tomorrow. Having a support system helped me through some of my darkest days.

Glen, on the other hand, probably didn't know how bad things were. He was my guy friend I would call whenever I was feeling down, and he would always cheer me up. He can always make me laugh. As a man, I too have trouble opening up to other men, so I never even told him he was part of my support group. We didn't have deep conversations, but we would talk about how messed up and hard life can be sometimes and then laugh about it. Glen grew up in a tough Toronto neighbour-hood and, against all odds, made it to the NHL. His story is incredible. He's one of the most kind, non-judgmental people I know. He's seen and been through a lot himself.

As the days ticked by, I continued to get stronger and stron-ger. It is ironic in a way that such a big source of my strength and support in recent years has come from the very hockey community that used to be my biggest source of shame and fear. It's like a bunch of us looked around one day and said, "Hey, wait a minute. Why the hell were we all so afraid of talking about our emotions?"

I give a lot of credit to those guys who ventured out before me with their stories. I am by no means the first athlete to go public with a mental health challenge. In hockey alone, there are quite a few guys who have made their mental illness and stories of trauma public. The list of those who came before me is long, and here are a couple.

Clint Malarchuk is a former NHL All-Star goaltender who has helped me through a lot with my mental illness. He's been a mentor and a great friend for me to lean on. He grew up with an abusive, alcoholic father, struggled with OCD as a teen and young adult, and when he was a member of the Buffalo Sabres in March 1989, a skate came up and cut his carotid artery and partially severed his jugular vein. The scene was horrific. If not for the quick-reacting Sabres trainer and medical staff, Clint would not have survived. As it was, it took near 300 stitches to sew up a six-inch gash on his neck. Ten days later, Clint was back on the ice playing.

The trauma of such a devastating injury did more than scar him physically. A self-admitted alcoholic, in 2008, Clint tried to take his life. He put a gun to his chin and pulled the trigger. Clint was intoxicated, and thankfully, he missed. A fragment of the bullet is still lodged in his brain. Clint checked himself into a dual diagnosis rehab clinic and got the help he needed. He dedicates himself today to helping others. He speaks and educates on mental health to anyone, and everyone, who will listen. He has been treated for alcoholism, OCD, anxiety, depression and PTSD. His book, *The Crazy Game*, is a riveting best-seller. Clint has also received an honorary doctorate from Nipissing University in North Bay, Ontario.

There are so many more I could list, but lastly, I'll mention NHL goaltender Robin Lehner.

Robin is from Sweden, and since breaking in with the Ottawa Senators in 2010–11, he has played in the NHL with Buffalo, the Islanders, Chicago and Vegas. Just before the 2018–19 season, Robin opened up about his mental health, admitting that he battled ADHD, PTSD, is bipolar and had drug and alcohol addictions. "The drinking and pills I was taking were to bring me down and even me out," he wrote in the *Athletic*. "Nothing else worked to calm down my brain." He added, "I could not stand being alone in my brain at nighttime." Robin, too, wanted to end his life.

Robin came out of rehab during the summer of 2018 and was looking for a fresh start. He was a free agent, and nine teams expressed interest in his goaltending. Robin and his agent agreed that they would be completely transparent and told each of the nine teams that Robin had been in rehab for alcohol and drugs, that he was bipolar and suffered from mental health challenges. Seven of the nine teams immediately dropped out. One of the two teams left that didn't drop out was only interested in Robin with limitations.

Robin said thanks but no thanks and moved on. As I said, communication and transparency are of the utmost impor-tance, and if they don't understand, or don't try to understand, then those aren't "your people." That organization was not Robin's people.

New York Islanders general manager Lou Lamoriello and head coach Barry Trotz were his people, so Robin signed with them. They were understanding, worked with Robin, and he rewarded them with a fantastic season. Robin got the team into the playoffs and finished the season as one of the three contenders for the Vezina Trophy, awarded to the NHL's best goaltender. He and his goaltending partner, Thomas Greiss, shared the William M. Jennings Trophy for allowing the fewest goals in the NHL. More importantly to this story, Robin was awarded the NHL's Bill Masterton Trophy as the player who best exemplifies perseverance, sportsmanship and dedication to hockey.

Before a viewing audience in the millions at the NHL Awards in Las Vegas in June 2019, Robin blew the doors off the stigma of mental health in his acceptance speech for winning the Masterton when he finished by saying: "I'm not ashamed to say I'm mentally ill, but that doesn't mean mentally weak."

Just because a person is a professional athlete does not make them immune to mental illness. Mental illness can happen to any of us, at any time and at any age, but those between the ages of 12 and 24 are especially vulnerable. Mental illness is non-discriminating—it doesn't matter a person's gender, race, creed, age or economic background. It doesn't matter if a person is a lawyer, doctor, construction worker, retail worker or professional athlete. Brains are physical pieces of our bodies and they break.

According to the Canadian Mental Health Association,

more than 6.7 million Canadians are currently living with a mental health condition. That means that one in five Canadians has experienced a mental health challenge. When it comes to sport, that means 20 percent of players on any given championship team are likely suffering from a mental health condition. Every Stanley Cup winner, Super Bowl champion or World Series championship team statistically has 20 percent of its players suffering from mental illness, and guess what? They still won. So don't tell me you can't have a successful company or a successful team with a player or employee who has mental illness. Olympic swimmer Michael Phelps won 23 gold medals and has since publicly revealed that he suffers from depression. Twenty-three Olympic gold medals! He went up against the best athletes in the world in an extremely high-pressure situation. Don't try to tell me he is weak!

There are millions of us, including athletes, who battle with mental health. I truly got better when I found a PhD-educated therapist. Not just anyone—an OCD specialist who got their PhD specifically in that field. Some therapists feel they can treat OCD, but it takes a qualified, trained expert in this area if a person truly wants to win the battle. All therapists are not created equal. Similar to every hockey player not being Wayne Gretzky. There are good hockey players and ones that are not so good. The same goes for therapists.

If a person needs a therapist, I ask them to please do their research and not just go see anyone. There is no shame in asking friends and others qualified, including a GP, to help with a referral. The first therapist I went to see in Calgary didn't diagnose me properly, wasn't qualified in OCD to treat me, and it almost killed me. I hear this same story from a lot of other OCD sufferers who had the same thing happen to them. For the love of God, if a therapist isn't qualified to treat OCD, they need to refer the patient to someone who can. It can turn out badly, with deadly consequences. I would like to see a country-wide mental health therapist referral system. A heart surgeon shouldn't be doing knee surgeries, and a knee surgeon shouldn't be doing heart surgery. Similarly, a guidance counsellor shouldn't be treating OCD.

It took me over 10 years and five therapists after my diagnosis to finally find a therapist who knew what they were doing with OCD. From the time it started that night in 1994 in Washington, it was actually 13 years before I found the proper help!

You want to know why people kill themselves? Think about this:

It had been over 13 years since that night in Washington when my OCD started.

It was over 10 years from the day I was diagnosed in my apartment in Vancouver.

I'd seen five different therapists and been on four different medications.

I'd spent over $20,000 on therapists and treatment.

All before I accidently stumbled onto the proper therapist and treatment by pure luck.

That's why the suicide rate is so astronomically high, especially during these difficult times.

A lot of the problems start with our education system. Teach our children about mental health in school. The vast majority of mental illnesses start between the ages of 12 and 24. By not educating our children, we are failing. A 2017 study by the

Centers for Disease Control and Prevention shows that suicide rates for those between 10 and 24 years of age were up 56 percent! Ten-year-olds have been taking their lives and we don't have mandatory mental health education in our school systems! The concept that discussing suicide leads to more suicides has to end. If someone is struggling, it's the first question I ask. I need to know so I can help them. It's too late to find out at their funeral. For every youth suicide, another child has been failed. Give them the information through our education system. They want it, need it, and it may save a life.

Mental health is *health*. That's why it's imperative to have mental health education in our schools. We are so uninformed, and it destroys lives. I had no idea what to do about my own treatment and even where to start to look for help. The vast majority of people suffer for 8 to 10 years before getting the proper help. I was one of those people. I was diagnosed at 24, and at 34 I was relapsing time and time again. I had no idea where to find the proper therapy, and not much has changed. For the general public, it's a dart tossed at a dartboard.

My daughter is a prime example. She's doing incredibly

well—proof that early diagnosis, education and talking about mental health in the home from an early age works. She's studying to be a teacher. She still struggles with her OCD at times, but she never got to that hopeless place I got to. It breaks my heart to know that there is a kid out there somewhere who has diagnosable OCD and has no idea what is going on in his or her head. If my daughter and I hadn't talked about mental health in our home, she would have suffered like I did, not knowing what was going on. Who knows what she could have done in that state of mind. Most people I know who have OCD have made at least one attempt on their life.

Educating people on suicide, including children, will not create more suicide or put ideas in a person's head. In fact, it's the opposite. Have open dialogue and let people know that if they are ever thinking of harming themselves, it's going to be okay and we will help them find a professional. I want to know if my child or friend is suicidal, because then I can do something about it and get them the help they need. The roots of failure of our school system not educating on mental health run deep from generation to generation. My mom didn't know what to do, my teammates didn't know what to do, and I certainly didn't know what to do. If I could have known what it was in my brain that broke that night in Washington, I would have gone for help the next day. I certainly wouldn't have ended up on the back roads two months later in Kamloops, trying to end my life.

In getting diagnosed, there was no magic fix. I had a long way to go to recover. Someone once told me that mental health is a marathon, not a sprint, and they were so right. I needed to unravel the giant ball of yarn that was woven inside my brain from not getting an early diagnosis. When a person is diagnosed with cancer, the best chance of recovery is from early diagnosis. Mental health is no different. It's so much easier to treat in the early stages. Cancer at Stage 4 is not good. Early diagnosis at Stage 1 is the easiest to treat. Same as if the thought of suicide and suicidal ideation is in Stage 4. It's a lot of work to pull a person back from that. I was at that stage and almost didn't make it.

It also goes beyond education; social and economic stereotypes don't help either. Unhealthy ideals about masculinity are a major contributor to men's mental health issues in society. Men have the most trouble opening up and telling someone they're struggling mentally. I know how hard it can be. I learned about masculinity and how to be a man on a bus between the ages of 16 and 19 in the Western Hockey League. A person can only imagine the things that I was shown back then. I felt I always had to suck it up, to never show emotion or affection at any time, and that showing any type of vulnerability was weak.

Well, where did that get me?

If I had been successful in an attempt to end my life, do you think my masculine male buddies would have come to my funeral and said, "Wow, what a man Corey was. He sucked it up. He didn't talk about his emotions. He went out like a man."

Not a chance. They would've all said, "Oh my God, why didn't he talk to me? Why didn't he tell somebody?"

The suicide rates for middle-aged men between the ages of 35 and 50 are off the charts. I attribute it to stigma, not having mental health education in our school system and the masculine idea that getting help by being vulnerable somehow makes a man weak.

I encourage my male brethren to please get help if they need it. The thought that getting professional help for the mind makes a man less of a man is ridiculous. I know how deeply rooted toxic masculinity can be. Hell, I still battle with my ideas of masculinity at times. But if you're still hard-headed, or you're worried about what people will think of you, or you're still holding onto those values that we were all taught 40, 20 or even 10 years ago about masculinity, then I'll just leave you with this:

This book is about suffering. There's no way around it. For years, I suffered terribly because I did not know what was wrong with me. But do you know what thought causes me the most pain? Do you know what is actually worse than the endless, ceaseless, bottomless loop of anger, anxiety, shame and torment that I would spiral into?

It is one simple *what if?*

And it is actually 100 times worse than my OCD spirals.

What if you had succeeded? What if you didn't hit the brakes that night in Kamloops? What if you weren't here anymore? What if you had missed all the beauty and love and precious moments with your children? What if you were just another statistic? Another newspaper headline. Another big, tough, courageous guy who suffered in silence. Another guy who is gone.

I am still here.

I am not okay. Maybe I will never be. But I am still here.

16

Sometimes, if you are lucky enough, you will have a moment of clarity in your life when you almost step outside of your body and see what a precious gift life can be. I had one of those moments a few years ago at Joe Louis Arena in Detroit. I was sitting there in that iconic building, watching as the crowd stood up, pumping their fists in the air, singing along to a song we'd all heard a million times before.

Just a city boy, born and raised in South Detroit.

He took the midnight train going anywhere.

I had to laugh at the irony. I was there watching my son and his youth hockey team belting out "Don't Stop Believin'" at the top of their lungs. All those kids were born around the year 2000. The song had been a hit for Journey in 1981. But in the world of hockey, it's timeless.

We were in Detroit for a travel tournament. It was the last season the Red Wings would ever play at the Joe before it was torn down. I wanted to get the boys into a Red Wings game to experience the electrifying environment it had to offer. The Joe was a historic building. It had all the character of an Original Six NHL barn with an atmosphere you can only create in the movies.

But it also just happened to be the arena where I had my first NHL start in 1993. Before all the darkness. Before the roller coaster. When I had my whole life planned out just perfectly.

Earlier that week, I had called Ken Holland, the Red Wings general manager. I told him the story and what a special moment it would be to get the boys to a game at the Joe. He was able to get us seats together up in the second level. There was more irony yet. We would be looking right down on the crease at the end of the ice where I once stood.

On the bus ride to the game through downtown Detroit with my son's team, I stood up in the aisle and told the boys how special this particular game was for me. I told them how I had played my first NHL game at the Joe in New York Rangers red, white and blue against these same Detroit Red Wings. They had a hell of a team back then, and the boys knew all the names: Fedorov, Probert, Yzerman.

I told the story of that game, two Original Six teams duking it out. I told them how I stopped Hall of Fame player Steve Yzerman on a breakaway in the second period and stoned another Hall of Famer, Sergei Fedorov, in close during overtime to preserve a 2–2 tie. I skated away that night having stopped 30 of 32 shots and was named the game's First Star.

As we entered the building, the kids were excited as hell and anxious to push through the crowd to get to our seats. I sat in the row directly behind my son because I knew I would get emotional. As I sat there, I couldn't help but stare out onto the ice, looking over top of my son's strawberry-blond hair, just like mine, at that same spot where it all started almost 24 years earlier.

I wiped a tear from my face as I flashbacked through all

the things I had suffered through to get here to this beautiful moment with him. If I had been successful in taking my life, that moment would never have existed. He never would have existed. All our happy times together on buses and long car rides going to and from tournaments, all our laughter and our tears in hockey rinks all over the country—all of it, gone. I would have been another statistic, another story of a young man gone too soon.

Instead, there I was in Detroit, full of life, and proud as hell with my son and his friends. The building rocked throughout the entire game and was just as loud as I remembered. When the final horn sounded, the Red Wings had won, and "Don't Stop Believin'" blared one last time over the loudspeakers. The kids went nuts, having the time of their lives. As the song played and I walked out of the Joe with my son for the final time ever, I put one arm around him. I pulled him towards me and hugged him as hard as I could.

I am forever thankful that even in my darkest days, I didn't give up. Life can bring us to our knees in a second. I know this. I've been there, but astonishingly, it can also bring us back from the brink. It can bring us back from love lost, from a job loss, from divorce or the death of a loved one, and it can even bring us back from the depths of fighting mental illness. Sometimes, the only solution is to just make it One More Day.

No matter how bad you feel, take it from me: I know it. I lived it. I understand.

I have felt the feeling that so many of us out there feel— and there are millions of us. That feeling of total despair. That feeling of complete darkness. That feeling of *I just can't go on anymore.*

But you can. The first step is to reach out for help. You can get better. You can find peace. I'm living proof of that.

There is a light, however faint, in all that darkness.

There is a light.

Epilogue

In this book, I tried to put the unspeakable into words. I did my damnedest to get everything that was going on in my head onto the page. But I realize that no matter how hard I try, it's next to impossible to describe the intricacies of mental health with simple language.

So if you still have questions, that's what this section is for. I am not a licensed professional. It's important to say that. But I wanted to make sure that this book had a resource at the end that readers (or even teachers and parents) could come back to again and again to understand the dynamics of OCD.

Of course, everyone is different, but my form of OCD is called Pure-O, and typically the content is sexually intrusive thoughts. I myself still find it embarrassing, shameful and humiliating to talk about. I have no idea why my content is sex-based while others may suffer from harm thoughts or something else. Nobody knows why. However, the best "in a nutshell" way I can explain having OCD is like this:

A person is driving down a two-way street, and the thought pops up, *What if I swerved my car into oncoming traffic?*

It's an impulsive, ridiculous thought that most of us have had in our lives while driving.

A person with a non-OCD brain would dismiss the thought as ridiculous, never think about it again and go on with their day. A person with an OCD brain would wonder why they thought something as heinous as that; they would get crushed with anxiety and ruminate for hours on what it meant. They would spend countless hours trying to make sure they didn't want to do that and hurt anyone. The questions *Why did I think that?* or *What if I did that?* would cycle again and again in their heads. A person with an OCD brain might even circle around the block and go back to make sure they didn't actually do it or run anyone over even though they know they didn't.

The rational side of their OCD brain would try to reassure them repeatedly that they would never drive into oncoming traffic, while the irrational side would try to convince them there is a tiny possibility of it happening, and that they better take extreme precautions so it doesn't ever happen. It becomes a massive fight in the OCD brain, with the two sides slugging it out. The irrational side creates an uncontrollable tsunami of panic and worry about a mythical event, and the rational side continually tries to reassure the person it hasn't done and won't ever do anything horrible like that. To stop the fight within their brain, a person with an OCD brain may just stop driving altogether and avoid the situation. They would never swerve into oncoming traffic, but the OCD brain wants to go to extreme cautions to make sure they won't.

This would be a Pure-O example of harm OCD.

I get calls regularly from people suffering with OCD asking for help, and it's all the same thing underneath. Their brains are lying to them, and it's only the content for them that is different from me. The OCD thoughts are intrusive, dark and horrible because they aren't true, and they cause panic attacks with great distress. It's like an annoying song a person can't get out of their head no matter how hard they try, except it's a thought that's horrific and on steroids.

Some people with OCD have obsessions and will act out physical compulsions to dispel the obsession. Obsessions are worry or fear thoughts that keep coming back. Compulsions are the actions a person with OCD may do to get relief to ensure their worry or fear doesn't actually come true. For example, when a person worries about getting sick from germs after touching a "contaminated" object such as a public door handle, they may repeatedly worry and ruminate for hours as to whether or not they will get themselves or someone else sick. This is the obsession. Then, in an effort to relieve the anxiety and feel better about the fear from the obsessive thought, they may wash their hands repeatedly to try to feel clean and therefore dispel the obsession. Hand washing would be the physical compulsion. If you are wondering if you have germ OCD, herein lies the difference: A person may wash their hands after touching a public door handle once or twice to avoid getting sick. The thought will go away and the person will go on with their day. However, an OCD person will get stuck on the thought of contamination for hours and wash their hands so many times that their hands may crack or bleed. They would not be able to stop it.

With Pure-O, like I have, it is a bit different. There are no outward physical compulsions after the obsessive thought. I do the compulsions in my head, which is why I am able to hide my OCD from anyone seeing it.

OCD can be categorized into four different areas:

1. Contamination (the fear of being dirty)
2. Aggression (fear of harming others)
3. Exactness (symmetry, counting and arranging)
4. Unacceptable taboo thoughts (Pure-O)

Pure-O has three very distinct categories:

1. Harm thoughts

2. Sexually intrusive

3. Religious

Harm thoughts may include a new mother having fearful thoughts and unwanted visions of harming her child.

Sexually intrusive thoughts can be anything from a person questioning their sexual orientation, questioning if they have an STD like HIV or not being able to stop unwanted graphic sexual images from repeatedly popping up in their brains.

Lastly, religious OCD can be something like seeking perfection in God's eyes; a person suffering from this might spend hours praying for fear of going to hell if they do anything wrong.

People with OCD are some of the most kind, empathetic and compassionate souls a person could ever meet. Sadly, we torture ourselves for not being "perfect" human beings, and the thought of hurting anything or anyone tears us up inside. That's why and how OCD attacks us. The difficulty of treating Pure-O is that the shame and embarrassment attached to the content makes these thoughts difficult for the sufferer to discuss. This type of OCD may be less well known than that of hand washers or checkers, but it is widespread within the OCD community. We all likely know someone who struggles with it; that person just may not have come forward. People with my type of OCD, like all other types of OCD, want 100 percent certainty that something terrible is not going to happen. Problem is, there is nothing in life that has 100 percent certainty.

My OCD will never be gone in my lifetime. It is not curable, but it is very treatable. There is no magic bullet or pill that will take it away, but there are therapies and medications that can drastically improve my life. I get therapy now for what is called ROCD—Relationship OCD. I have to be careful, as ROCD tries to confuse me into having unwanted intrusive relationship thoughts. It's still the same garbled content as all the other types of OCD, but the wrapping package has changed. This is why ongoing lifelong therapy is so important for me. Treatment teaches me how to stop it before it drags me deep down the rabbit hole time and time again. OCD is sneaky and hard to pinpoint at times. The help of a qualified therapist is crucial in the fight against it. Having any mental health issue can feel like being lost in a forest, not being able to find a way out. A therapist is a person in a helicopter who can get above the trees and guide you out of the forest.

Ultimately, what has made all the difference for me is a combination of medication and a therapy called ERP that changed my life. CBT was the first therapy I tried, and while it lessened my anxiety, it wasn't enough, and I was always on a path to relapse. In getting diagnosed, relapsing and going through my life experiences, I have come to learn that I will most likely be on medication for the rest of my life. My brain doesn't produce enough of a chemical called serotonin. It's what balances my anxiety levels and prevents my brain from being overwhelmed with anxiety.

There is a terrible stigma attached to medication, and I want to end that. I'm not sure what's worse—the stigma of having a mental health issue or the stigma attached to taking medication for our brains. I would not be alive if not for medication. I am 100 percent positive that I would have taken my own life. It took me a long time to get on medication because of the stigma and the myths I had heard about it. I thought somehow it made me weak if I took medication, and I would be less of a man.

Tough it out! Real men don't need meds, I thought. *A real man can do this on his own.*

So foolish. It took me until I was completely down on my knees to finally take the plunge and get on it. I started on medication a couple of months after diagnosis. It wasn't perfect, but it took the edge off. It wasn't a magic cure, but it helped enough that I could live life somewhat normally and my brain could accept the treatment. A person is not weak if they take medication. It helped me get through some really tough, dark days. I would never tell someone who has cancer or diabetes to not take their medication, so why would anyone tell a person with a mental health condition that it's okay not to take their medication? My brain doesn't produce enough serotonin. I need medication and therapy to increase those levels. How is that my fault, and why should I be stigmatized for it? Would it be better if I didn't take medication and be dead? I think not. I can't be a man if I'm dead.

Depression, anxiety, OCD—whatever is challenging a person, they need to do whatever they have to do to fight it. There is a better life out there. And the stigma towards medication has to end! I'm not pushing pharma. We still have a long way to go in research and development, but it shocks me that people will self-medicate with alcohol or street drugs, yet if you suggest prescription medication, they resist due to stigma. Medication alone is not enough, and therapy alone may not be enough, but a combination of therapy and the right medication can make all the difference.

I struggle to understand why, even though our brains are the most complex thing physically we have as humans, society will stigmatize and punish people when they break. Humans are not built perfectly, and there isn't a person out there whose brain is not susceptible to breaking. Just like an organ, a bone or a tendon, brains break down, and if a person's brain does break down, society adds stigma on top of it by denouncing people for taking medication to get better.

There is a long way to go with medications and research, but I see kids suffering severely with OCD and their parents won't give them medicine to help. If it was heart disease or diabetes, it is okay to take meds, but if it's a brain, why is it somehow different? Side effects suck, I'm not going to lie, but all medications carry side effects. I had zero quality of life when not medicated, so what's worse—a few side effects, compared to not being able to function at all, or worse yet, ending my life?

Medication alone is not enough for me. It's only part of the solution. A combination of therapy and medication is my best route of treatment. We should all be educated on this about mental health.

So how does one tell the difference between everyday worry or sadness and a serious, diagnosable mental health issue?

We all at some point in our lives will feel anxiety or some form of sadness, but we power through and can live our lives. While that sucks, and I feel for people who go through it, it's not clinical depression or a crippling mental health issue. It becomes a mental health issue when it keeps you from doing something you love or feeling joy in anything at all. That's when a person needs to reach out for help.

When a person suffers from anxiety or depression, it's their brain lying to them, and it creates chaos and confusion. Anxiety and depression make it difficult to make good decisions, especially when a person isn't aware that's what their brain is doing. I know personally that my brain will do this to me. It's just the way it functions and I need to be aware of its lying so I can battle my mental health issues. My OCD and ADHD will never be gone, but by managing them through self-care, therapy and medication, I can have just as good a quality of life as anyone else. It is not a life sentence, and I don't view it that way.

So what signs are there to look for in a person, and how do we help someone struggling with their mental health?

Here are some examples of what I have learned a mental health struggle may look like:

1. Sudden weight loss or weight gain
2. Sudden drop in grades or work ethic
3. Trouble focusing on a conversation
4. Withdrawing from family and friends/activities
5. Being late; making unexplained excuses
6. Feelings of worthlessness
7. Oversleeping / not sleeping
8. Complete loss of joy in anything and everything
9. Substance abuse

Disclaimer: These are only my opinion, and I am not a qualified therapist. It's best to talk to a qualified professional for more information.

If you see any of these signs in a friend, co-worker, spouse or child, it's a good idea to have a conversation with them. Simply ask if they are okay or if they want to talk. Let them know you are a safe, non-judgmental person who is there to listen. Encourage therapy and tell the person you are there for them if they want help. That person may not open up right away. It may be a week, a month or even a year, but if they want the help, they will open up eventually. You can't force anyone to get help. A good first step is to try and get the person to see their GP. They can get a therapist referral from there. If it's a child, that's different. A parent can take the child to a therapist with the consent of both parents. They too can start with asking their GP.

So how does a person talk to someone they suspect may be struggling?

Encourage therapy. Reassure them that help is available, that they will get better, that there is hope and help out there for them.

Listen without judgment. Judging someone can put them back into hiding for years. I'm not qualified to diagnose people, but I can listen, and I can listen without judgment. Sometimes, that's all that it takes. And encourage therapy.

Tell someone. If it gets serious enough, tell somebody who can help. Reach out, ask questions. Mental health takes a village, and we are all in this together

Do not point out how great their life is. Trust me, the person will already feel shitty enough for feeling the way they do. It's not in their control, and that's only going to make a person feel worse. Anyone could have pointed out how great my life was—Stanley Cup, Olympic medal, NHL career. It wouldn't have mattered. My brain was broken, and I needed professional help.

Please remember that if you are not a qualified therapist, it's best not to try to solve the person's problems; leave that to the professionals. Some people just want to talk and aren't looking for answers; they just want to get it out. Let the qualified therapists help them. I am not qualified to help someone with their problems, but I can listen and point a person in the right direction.

What can a person do to take care of their own mental health? I have learned several self-care strategies for maintaining one's mental health:

Eat healthy. As a professional athlete, I was always taught that whatever I put in my body was to make me bigger, stronger and faster, and as a result, I'd be a better player. I wasn't taught that what I put in my stomach goes directly to my brain. When a person is driving their car and it's low on fuel, they put gas in the car. If they put a can of Coke in the gas tank, the car's not going to go anywhere. The body has the same principle. If we put good fuel in the car, the car is going to run. If we put good fuel in our bodies, our brains are going to work, and our bodies will function a lot better.

Get regular sleep. If I don't get enough sleep, I'm an anxious mess, and it can fuel my OCD. Our brains need the rest time to recharge.

Prioritize physical fitness. Exercise is not an option for me. After I was finished playing hockey, I thought I would never exercise again, but I quickly discovered that it is not an option for someone with mental illness. I should broaden that—it's actually not an option for any of us. Our brains need the endorphins; they need exercise to be able to function properly. When I feel my anxiety mounting or feel depression coming on, I know I have to up my exercise.

Take a break from social media. The kids call it FOMO—Fear of Missing Out. If I set my phone aside for 15 minutes, the anxiety I get from thinking I missed a text or a call is off the charts. That tells me I need to set aside my phone a few times a day and not look at it. Take that time out.

Stay connected with others and don't withdraw. Connecting with others is so important. If a person sees somebody withdrawing, help them connect. I talked about my support group of two or three people who I lean on. Each of them knows that I have mental health issues. If I start to withdraw, they'll come to me and get me going again.

Do relaxation and meditation exercises. A simple exercise a person can do is to close their eyes and take five deep breaths. They should notice they will feel more relaxed after a few minutes of this. There are great calming apps available that help you do just that.

Keep a journal. Journalling daily about gratitude and what you're thankful for is a great way to help with mental health. I try to journal every night. There are some days when I can't think of anything to write, but I always find something. No matter how my day has gone, there's something to be thankful for.

Use time management for stress. Whether it's a meeting, a class or playing a sport, time management is crucial for mental health. This is how my game day was structured when I was playing hockey. My time management routine for a 7:00 p.m. game would look like this:

5:00: Get the sticks ready that I was going to use for the game.

5:15: Stretch and do some visualization exercises.

5:30: Power play / penalty kill meeting with coaches.

5:45: Do something fun to de-stress, like kick a soccer ball or toss a football around.

6:00: Put on my equipment

6:30: Go on ice for warmup

6:50: Coach would come in and go over some details

7:00: Game time

Why was my game-day routine so structured? It's time management. The game is stressful and if I didn't prepare properly, our team could be down 3–0 before I knew it. It's no different no matter what a person does for a living—an important meeting, an important test. Time management skills are crucial for mental health.

Do something you enjoy every day. Take some time every day to do something fun. Whether it's drawing, throwing a baseball around, calling a friend—it doesn't matter. It's important for your mind.

Talk and talk and talk. Talk to friends, family, anyone you trust who can help. You will find it amazing, when they open up, how many others will have been through the same issues as you. We can't see if a person is fighting their mental health, and the only way to help someone is if they say something.

Another disclaimer: Please know these are not treatment suggestions for diagnosable mental health issues. These are only maintenance suggestions anyone can do. Suggesting that anyone can cure a severe mental health issue this way would be both dangerous and irresponsible.

*

Mental illness is far more prevalent than most people realize. It is estimated that

- 10–20% of our youth are affected by mental illness.

- 5% of males and 12% of females ages 12 to 19 have experienced a severe depression.

- by the age of 40, close to 50% of the population will have or have had a battle with mental illness.

- suicide accounts for 24% of deaths among 15- to 24-year-olds and is among the leading causes of death, second only to accidents.

- suicide accounts for 16% of deaths among 25- to 44-year-olds, both male and female.

- 75% of completed suicides are male and more than 4,000 people die by suicide each year.

It is an epic crisis, and something needs to change.

What is extremely maddening to me is that only one in five youths who need mental health services receives help. In fact, close to half of those who have suffered from depression or anxiety have never sought medical help.

The word *suicide* can no longer be taboo. We need to start the hard conversation and ask people if they are considering self-harm. Having people feel as though they should hide in shame for thinking those thoughts will only drive them further into the underground. If someone is talking about taking their life or harming themselves, please don't shame them for having those thoughts. TELL someone that can help, and for God's sake, don't leave them alone to be by themselves. Tell a parent, an adult, call a therapist or their doctor.

And if you are that person thinking those thoughts, and you're afraid to say something, all I can do, for the last time, is beg you to tell someone, *anyone*, these three words:

I need help.

There are 60,000 words in this book. If you hold on to just three words from this book, please make it those three.

Acknowledgements

In writing this book, I'm grateful for the wise advice and support from my agent Jeff Jacobson, Kevin Shea and the team at HarperCollins. I had the privilege of working with Sean Conboy at the *Players' Tribune* on "Dark, Dark, Dark, Dark, Dark, Dark, Dark, Dark." The overwhelming response to the *Players' Tribune* article both surprised and touched me beyond words. So it was an even greater privilege to work with Sean again on this book, and I appreciate his patience and expertise in helping to tell my story. To my teammates and friends who reached out to me in my darker days, your care and compassion meant a lot, even if I may not have known it at the time.

For the families who are heartbroken from the tragic loss of loved ones to suicide, we are in a club together that we don't want to belong to, that we didn't ask to be in, but please know you are never alone and I am with you.

To my mother, Cheryl, my father, Ken, and my brother, Stacey—I am forever grateful to you for your love, your support and for never judging me. My love for you all is eternal. You taught me kindness, empathy and resilience. You were always there for me in my darkest days and saved me more times than you will ever know.

To my children, Alexa, Hayden and Farrah—you are the loves of my life, I live for you and I do everything I do for you. My hope is that at the end of my time on earth you will be able to see me not only as your father, but as a man who used his life for a greater purpose. A man who lived the best way he knew how and treated others with kindness, compassion and empathy. Through it all, the only thing that will matter to me is for you to be able to say that you were proud of me, and proud that I was your dad. You will forever be my Posse. I love you with all my being.